THE SOUTH WEST COAST
A PHOTOGRAPHIC HISTORY

THE SOUTH WEST COAST

A PHOTOGRAPHIC HISTORY

CHRIS THURMAN

TEMPUS

Frontispiece: St Michael's Mount in Cornwall, 1985. Photographed in hazy sunshine, this viewpoint shows clearly the causeway which links the mainland to the small island. Further details of this historic area are given in chapter eleven.

This is the third book by Chris Thurman which Tempus has published. The others are:
London's River – IBSN 0 7524 2595 I
Essex Thames-side – ISBN 0 7524 3232 X

First published 2006

Tempus Publishing Ltd
The Mill, Brimscombe Port
Stroud, Gloucestershire GL5 2QG
www.tempus-publishing.com

© Chris Thurman, 2006

The right of Chris Thurman to be identified as the Author of this work has been asserted by him in accordance with the Copyrights, Designs and Patents Act 1988.

British Library Cataloguing in Publication Data.
A catalogue record for this book is available from the British Library.

ISBN 0 7524 3961 8

Typesetting, design and origination by Tempus Publishing.
Printed in Great Britain

Acknowledgements

To my wife Gill for her support while producing this book. To Joyce Brown, the Local and Naval Studies Librarian at Plymouth Central Library, for her help in identifying the buildings in the 1930s photographs and to the people in the Lifeboat shop in Ilfracombe. Many of the modern photographs of Dorset and South Devon were taken while Gill and I were staying with John and Margaret Heil. I also wish to thank Katherine Burton of Tempus for her initial enthusiasm for this book and Ed Palmer and Emma Jackson for seeing the project through to publication.

References

I have referred to many different websites, booklets and leaflets during the preparation of this book and the *Pears Cyclopaedia* is always good for finding dates. My most used books have been the green Michelin guide to the South West; the AA Ordnance Survey leisure guide to Cornwall, the AA *Illustrated Guide to Britain*, published in 1971 and finally the Cornwall and Devon books from the Arthur Mee series on the King's England, first published in 1937 and 1938 respectively.

Contents

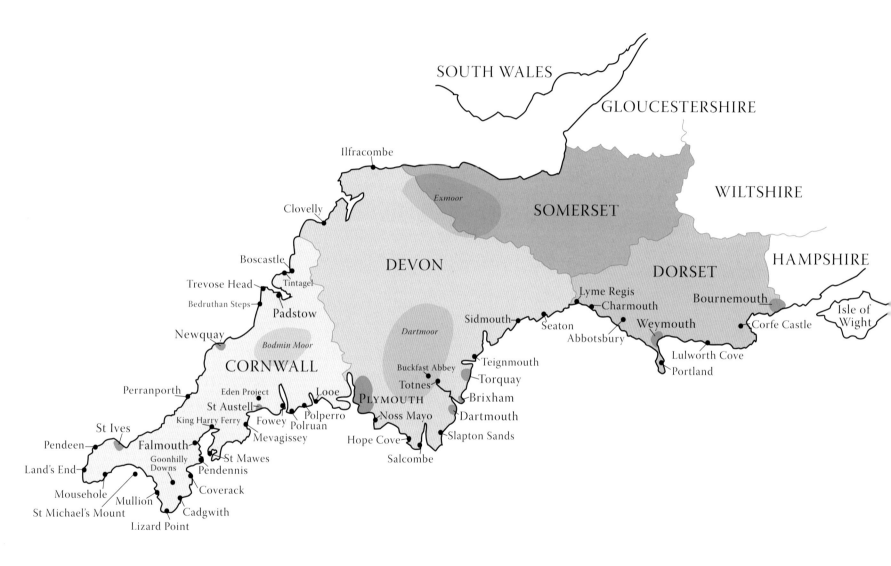

SOUTH WALES

GLOUCESTERSHIRE

WILTSHIRE

SOMERSET

Exmoor

HAMPSHIRE

DEVON

DORSET

Ilfracombe

Clovelly

Lyme Regis

Boscastle

Charmouth

Bournemouth

Trevose Head

Tintagel

Sidmouth

Weymouth

Corfe Castle

Isle of
Wight

Bedruthan Steps

Seaton

Padstow

Abbotsbury

Newquay

Dartmoor

Lulworth Cove

Bodmin Moor

Portland

CORNWALL

Teignmouth

Buckfast Abbey

Perranporth

Eden Project

Looe

Torquay

St Austell

PLYMOUTH

Totnes

St Ives

King Harry Ferry

Fowey

Polperro

Polruan

Brixham

Pendeen

Mevagissey

Noss Mayo

Dartmouth

Falmouth

Hope Cove

Slapton Sands

Land's End

Goonhilly
Downs

St Mawes

Salcombe

Pendennis

Mousehole

Coverack

Mullion

St Michael's Mount

Cadgwith

Lizard Point

Introduction

The South West was always a popular holiday destination for my parents in the 1930s, indeed they had even undertaken a day trip from East Ham (at that time in Essex, now part of Greater London) utilising a return fare which I think was described as a 'Sunday League'. Thus it was fairly inevitable that as a young photographer with a brand new camera we went there for a holiday. This was in 1955, and there are a couple of shots from that trip included in this book. Like many other Britons at that time we continued to take many more holidays in that region in the 1950s and 1960s.

However, as time passed it became clear that some of the things I had photographed had changed. Change is most noticeable in terms of fashion and cars, but as will be evident from the comments below, and the photographs contained within this book, there are many other changes. While many books show places as they were, say, 100 years ago, this book is different. It looks at more recent changes; changes that have occurred within the lifetimes of millions of people.

The Book's Coverage

The photographs follow a coastal route. This starts at Bournemouth and continues along the South Coast to Weymouth, Torquay, St. Mawes and so to Lands End. At this point it then continues along the Cornish North Coast. Cornwall's North Coast is the Atlantic Ocean, and as the photographs will show, it is quite different from the county's southern coast.

Specifically the three counties covered in this book are:

	Area in sq kms	Population
Dorset		
County Council	2542	395,000
Bournemouth UA	46	164,000
Poole UA	65	138,000
Total including UA's	2,653	697,000
Devon		
County Council	6,564	710,000
Torbay UA	63	131,000
Plymouth UA	80	164,000
Total including UA's	6,707	1,005,000
Cornwall		
County Total	3,563	508,000

UA = Unitary Authority. For instance, from a geographical point of view, Torquay is obviously part of Devon, but in terms of local government it operates outside the Council as its administrative functions are contained within the Torbay Unitary Authority. For hundreds of years, Bournemouth was part of Hampshire, but as a result of the 1972 local government re-organisations it became part of Dorset before it achieved Unitary Authority status.

Three of the major towns in these counties are noted in the above table: namely, Bournemouth, Poole and Plymouth. Other large towns in the region include Weymouth, Torquay and Newquay.

The towns and villages beside the coast include the following categories:

1 Seaside resorts which had developed prior to the 'railway age', such as Weymouth and Sidmouth.
2 Seaside resorts which developed after the coming of the railways.
3 Fishing communities. Some of these are substantial, such as Brixham, while others are very small, such as those in Cornwall (Coverack, for instance).
4 Ports used (either currently or in the past) by the Royal Navy, primarily Weymouth (Portland) and Plymouth.
5 Commercial ports. These may be for freight or for cross channel passenger ferries.

Industry

There are (or have been) many important industries in this area, such as:

1 Tourism
2 Fishing
3 Commercial (freight and passengers) and Royal Naval ports.
4 Clay quarrying
5 Tin mining.

Photographs dealing with all these different industries appear in the book, and for the most part comments about the industries are contained within the captions of the appropriate photographs. During the period covered by the photographs there have been economic changes, such as the transfer of the Brixham fishing fleet to a brand new harbour.

Opposite: Brixham, 1966. This scene is no longer possible as the fishing fleet now ties up in the outer harbour which is not accessible to the general public: see chapter seven for more details.

Tourism

The economic health of the South West is much dependent upon tourism, and it has always been a popular holiday destination. The earliest resorts developed in the Regency period, such as Weymouth and Sidmouth, but since then their evolution has reflected changes in modes of transport. Much of the region's subsequent success followed the development of the railways during the nineteenth century and the general increasing prosperity in the country which gave many people the opportunity to take holidays. Thereafter the next boost to the region's holiday success was the arrival of the motor car, which gave people the opportunity to visit/explore resorts that were inaccessible to railways.

The South West continued to be a popular holiday destination throughout the early part of the twentieth century until well into the 1960s. Once the post-war petrol rationing had ceased in May 1950, people started to make their journeys to the South West by car, and I can well remember the horrendous traffic jams at Honiton and on the Exeter bypass at the junction by the Countess of Wear public house. However, as can be seen in one of the Torquay photographs, trains continued to provide a vital passenger link to this area. In the 1950s, the vast majority of holidays taken by Britons were in this country. This might be for a fortnight or only for one week. However, perhaps the biggest drawback of an English holiday is the weather, with periods of cold and rain. While the South West is one of the warmest places in the UK, it is also one of the wetter areas.

By the early 1960s the popularity of holidays in English seaside resorts started to change and once again a transport revolution was an essential factor. This was the arrival of jet powered passenger aircraft which meant that Mediterranean countries were within some two hours flight time. Allied to this faster transport was a major marketing development – the package holiday, where for a single price a customer could buy a flight, hotel accommodation and the transfers between the destination airport and the hotel. Hotel prices in countries such as Spain were cheaper than in the UK, and in addition a tour operator could negotiate favourable terms from the overseas hotel owner and from the airline operator. Package holidays to places in Spain (such as Majorca, Costa Brava, Costa del Sol) were not only price competitive, but good summer weather was virtually guaranteed. The boom in overseas holidays had started and the losers were the traditional English seaside resorts. Just to give one simple figure: between 1971 and 1998 the number of trips abroad made by UK residents increased 7.7 times (or, put another way, by 669 per cent).

Ironically, the most recent development in transport may be about to benefit areas such as the South West. This is the growth of low priced 'no frills' airlines which often use smaller, out-of-the-way airports.

When the photographs of Weymouth were taken in 1963, holidays were still taken to a great extent in this country. In 1966, Torquay was still benefiting from people choosing to stay at home; perhaps taking a second, shorter, holiday in this country while taking the main one in places such as Spain, Italy or (later) Greece.

The more commercial of the English seaside resorts have responded to this changing situation in a number of ways:

> The construction of marinas and improvements to yacht mooring facilities.
> The construction of conference centres.
> The construction of leisure and artistic centres such as the Tate Gallery in St Ives.
> An emphasis on holiday facilities for the whole year, and on taking shorter breaks.

This latter point is very relevant. It is clearly important for businesses in the tourist industry to be able to utilise their assets as much as possible throughout the whole year, thereby maintaining a steady income over the twelve months. This can be done in several ways: mid-week special offers, weekend 'bargain breaks', special interest weeks and so on. In this context, the emergence of a large 'grey' (defined by hair colour) market over the past couple of decades has been a particular boon to hotels and other companies in the tourism industry as this group of people are able to visit tourist areas outside the peak periods (determined by factory closures and school holidays).

As late as the 1950s the norm for most people was two weeks holiday per year and this was taken in either July or August. However, as the following figures for the South West show, while the summer is still the most popular time, visits are indeed spread throughout the year. In 2003, the proportion of all holiday visits to the South West taken in the first quarter of the year (January to March) was 19 per cent, 26 per cent in the second quarter, 33 per cent in the third quarter and finally 22 per cent in the period October to December.

The result is that seaside resorts that have allowed for this change in social behaviour continue to do well, and attract visitors throughout the year. Indeed this book contains photographs taken in mid-summer in Weymouth and Torquay, in the autumn in Newquay, and at Christmas in Bournemouth.

One final development in holidays should also be noted. This is the growth of 'activity' holidays, and it touches upon the South West in at least two ways: surfing and walking (including the popularity of the South West coastal path).

Manifestations of Change

The changes of the past few decades which can be observed in the photographs in this book can be grouped together under at least three broad headings: economic (already referred to), fashion and cars.

Changes in fashion are an obvious way to measure the passing of years. These can be either in clothing or in hairstyles. One obvious change has been the move towards a much more casual way of dressing, particularly when at the seaside. This is even true of men's clothing – in some of the earlier photographs men can be seen wearing jackets and ties on a warm summer's day. And as for headwear, there was never a baseball cap to be seen!

The design of cars has changed considerably over the years covered by this book (as has their reliability). This can be shown by a simple statistic – between 1961 and 2001 the number of cars on the road increased by more than four times (or, put another way, by 324 per cent). The much lighter traffic usage at the beginning of the period is noticeable in two ways – cars parked in places which would now not be allowed and the lack of any single or double lines on the side of the road.

South West Coastal Path

This path did not exist as a complete entity in its own right when the first photographs in this book were taken. It has been established as one of the country's long distance paths, and is indeed 630 miles long, wending its way from Poole in Dorset to Minehead in Somerset. The South West coast is full of cliffs and thus there are many ups and downs – indeed the path's website suggests that the totality of these ups is equal to three times the height of Mount Everest. Overall, the photographs in this book stay with the coastal areas, but there is the occasional detour inland.

The path goes through many different towns, fishing villages and past some truly wonderful coastal scenery. The coastal path crosses many different rock formations but a description of the geology is beyond the remit of this book. An overview of the geology of this area, the different rocks, how and when they were formed, is given on the South West Coastal Path website.

A wide spectrum of activities and seascapes are reflected by the photographs gathered in this book. Inevitably, having been taken over a period extending beyond five decades, they also portray social and economic change.

Chris Thurman, MBE, ARPS

March 2006

CHAPTER 1

Bournemouth

THE SOUTH WEST COAST
A PHOTOGRAPHIC HISTORY

Previous page: It was (maybe still is) a tradition that some people go swimming in the sea on Christmas morning. It was (and maybe still is) part of this tradition that the swimmers dress up in old-fashioned swimwear. This is how it looked on Christmas Day in 1978. They stayed in the sea for only a short period of time, which was not surprising, as it was quite cold.

The Victorian- or Edwardian-style, bathing costumes worn by these people hark back to Bournemouth's early days. Some 200 years ago Bournemouth hardly existed, but like many seaside resorts, it developed in the nineteenth century with the coming of the railways and the generally higher prosperity of the later part of the nineteenth century. While there was still extreme poverty in the big industrial areas, nevertheless there were many thousands of people who were able to take advantage of the travel opportunities brought about by the 'railway age'.

Above: Boscombe Pier, 1977. Bournemouth is fortunate in that it actually has two piers, just over a mile apart. This photograph shows Boscombe Pier, which is situated on the eastern side of Bournemouth, with the coast continuing eastwards towards Hengistbury Head. To the right on the Head, and on the horizon, is the outline of the Isle of Wight.

Altogether, Bournemouth has seven miles of beach and is comprised of the town itself as well as Boscombe and Southbourne. Indeed, the entire 'conurbation' also includes Christchurch and Poole.

Left: Bournemouth Pier, 1984. This view is looking west towards Poole, and the headland in the distance is the Dorset coast going towards Swanage and Studland Bay. Bournemouth (like Torquay – see chapter six) is one of the classic English seaside resorts

Pleasure piers, as they were called, were a feature of many British seaside resorts and were built during the later part of the nineteenth century. They were meant to give a point of focus to the resort as well as providing revenue for the owners through amenities such as cafés, amusement machines and sometimes small music halls. A further source of revenue might be an admission charge to the pier. Even in winter the pier continues to meet customers' needs and provides shelter to enable visitors to enjoy the winter sunshine. The longest pier in the UK is at Southend-on-Sea, and is featured in my book *Essex Thames-side*.

Taken in 1977, this photograph shows one part of Bournemouth's city centre. The low long building on the centre right is the Royal Bath Hotel, a nineteenth-century building of five-star luxury which was originally owned by the Russell-Cotes, whose museum and art gallery is situated nearby. The tall blocks of flats (apartments) are an indicator that Bournemouth has successfully moved from being a resort established in the railway era to one meeting modern requirements, and it is indeed one of the largest seaside resorts in England.

To be successful, resorts nowadays have to offer facilities such as conference centres, and Bournemouth has this modern facility. Resorts also have to cater for all seasons and the next few photographs were all taken over the Christmas period.

However, even at Christmas, the weather is not always cold and dull, and sometimes the sun can shine. These four ladies are enjoying some Christmas sunshine in 1977.

These surfers were photographed
from Bournemouth Pier at
Christmas 1977.

There is a logical explanation as to why a man in a three-piece suit should be on a beach: it is Christmas 1977, and this photograph was taken just before lunch on Christmas Day. He is almost certainly spending Christmas in a hotel, and he is well dressed as a Christmas Day luncheon in a hotel would be a fairly formal occasion.

Was this metal detector a Christmas present? These two people are surveying Bournemouth beach at Christmas 1977 to see if they could find anything of interest. Even the dog appears to be wondering what is happening.

Jon Pertwee, 1976. Jon Pertwee had made his name participating in a number of different British radio comedies, but he subsequently achieved further success playing Doctor Who in a British sci-fi television programme called, appropriately, *Doctor Who*. This photograph was taken during a cabaret performance. Live entertainment on stage is one of the traditions of the British seaside holiday.

CHAPTER 2

Corfe Castle to Weymouth

Previous page: Corfe Castle, 1951. Corfe Castle is one of the most impressive sights between Bournemouth and Weymouth, although not on the direct route. The castle dates back to the eleventh century, and became a ruin in 1646 as a result of the Civil War between the monarchists (popularly known as the 'Cavaliers') and the parliamentary forces led by Oliver Cromwell (the 'Roundheads'). The general view is still much like this today, but there are many differences of detail reflecting the changes which have taken place over the past five decades.

Two reminders from the early 1950s are the young couple (left hand pavement) who are no doubt dressed in the casual clothes of the day, while the two cars are a Vauxhall estate and an Austin saloon. Nowadays, a set of traffic lights dominates the scene from this viewpoint and the road is littered with a variety of white and yellow lines; these changes are a direct result of the increase in road traffic over this time.

Both pubs still exist – the Greyhound pub at the road junction and the Bank's Arms on the right (not named in this photograph). Both pubs are shown as being owned by Strong and Co. of Romsey. I well remember the placards that used to be beside the main roads entering this area saying that 'You are now entering Strong country'. Strong was a brewing company located in Romsey, but it ceased to exist as an independent company in the 1960s (becoming part of the Whitbread group). The beer market continued to grow throughout the 1970s, reaching a peak in 1979, and the brewery continued to remain active throughout this period. It was closed in 1980 following the downturn in beer sales. Furthermore, it produced traditional ales and the market was turning rapidly to lager.

Another indicator of change is that now no brewer's name appears outside either pub. Following the recommendations of the Monopolies and Mergers Commission in 1989, and the subsequent 'Beer Orders', there were substantial changes in pub ownership, and the national brewers, like Whitbread, were particularly affected.

Above: One of the themes of this book is how formal people used to be when in holiday locations, one example being men wearing jackets and ties. In this view of Lulworth cove, taken in the summer of 1963, there is a small girl wearing a tailored outer coat.

Above: Lulworth Cove, seen here in 1959, is one of the most remarkable places on the coast between Bournemouth and Weymouth. The sea has managed to make a break between the solid cliffs and then has etched out the cove from softer inland rocks.

Above: Weymouth, 1963. Weymouth is situated in the middle of a wide bay, and this photograph shows the view to the east. It was taken in the early morning, looking left along the promenade before the beaches became crowded with either holiday-makers staying in Weymouth or day-trippers. The coach is part of the local transport system and the clock was erected to mark the Golden Jubilee of Queen Victoria. Also visible are part of Weymouth Pier, which no longer exists, and a beach photographer's tented booth.

A traditional feature of many British seaside resorts is a Punch and Judy stall, an example of which is seen here on Weymouth's beach in 1963. It is a glove puppet show and designed to appeal to children. It is interesting to look at the people's clothes and to reflect on how different they are from today's fashions.

Opposite below: Weymouth, 1963. Weymouth is one of the few seaside resorts in this country whose popularity pre-dates the coming of the railways. It has also been an important harbour for many centuries and both of these aspects are shown in this photograph. In the forefront is a traditional seaside promenade, and then there is a typical crowded beach scene so typical of English seaside resorts at peak summer periods during the 1950s and early 1960s. The holiday aspects of Weymouth are shown in this chapter while photographs of the harbour are contained in the next chapter, thereby highlighting the two different economic aspects of this town.

Weymouth came to prominence as a seaside resort through the visits of King George III. He made his first visit in 1789 and then returned some fourteen times during the period up to 1805. He stayed in the 'Gloucester Lodge', which was built by his brother, Henry, the 1st Duke of Gloucester and Edinburgh, following the latter's visit to Weymouth in 1780. The coming of railways to Weymouth helped to further its position as a leading resort, which it has retained to this day. The promenade shelters date from the Victorian period.

Most of the photographs that follow were taken in 1963, when most British people still took their holidays at home. However, it was at this time that packaged holidays (incorporating both airfares and the costs of hotel accommodation) to places in Spain and Italy began to be popular.

This kiosk on the beach is selling ice cream, teas and other refreshments. It is 1963 and the man is dressed pretty formally, wearing both a long sleeve shirt and a tie, and yet he is presumably on holiday. On the other hand, standing next to him, is a girl in a swimsuit.

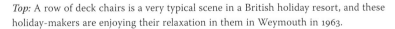

Top: A row of deck chairs is a very typical scene in a British holiday resort, and these holiday-makers are enjoying their relaxation in them in Weymouth in 1963.

Above: Weymouth, 1963. The most remarkable feature of this photograph is the clothes. There are two boys with tailored short trousers and ankle socks, and several of the men are wearing jackets – one indeed has a suit.

Top: Weymouth, 1963. This and the photograph below form a link with the following chapter dealing with Weymouth Harbour.

Above: This photograph, taken in 1963, shows the proximity of the harbour to the pleasure beach. Although mid-summer, the people walking onto the beach are dressed for cool weather. The large building in the centre and the buildings on the right are still there, albeit they have been rejuvenated. The ship moored in Weymouth harbour is the *St Patrick*.

Previous Page: Weymouth, 1963. This ship is called the *St Patrick* and was one of the passenger ferries operating out of Weymouth. The three cars parked right beside the ship are a Ford Prefect, a Ford Zephyr and an Austin Cambridge.

Cross channel shipping services have been a feature of Weymouth harbour for over two centuries. The service developed further after the railway was extended into a dockside ferry terminal (see later photographs) and in 1889 the Great Western Railway, which had developed these dockside facilities, commenced its regular services to the Channel Islands using its own boats. Following the nationalisation of the railways, these services were taken over by British Rail and this service continued until 1990 under the name 'Sealink'.

Today this service is provided by Condor Ferries, which started operating from Weymouth in 1987. They use Hydrofoils, which carry both passengers and cars, and currently (early 2006), they offer three services – to Guernsey, Jersey and St Malo in Brittany.

Weymouth, 1963. The port of Weymouth has a very long and distinguished history. There are records of Roman galleys travelling in this area, and certainly by the Middle Ages it was a very busy seaport. This activity has included cargo, fishing and passenger traffic. In this view, the cargo ship *Elk* is moored on Custom House Quay. As can be seen in this and later photographs, the railway reached right into the harbour and the dockside.

Opposite top: Weymouth, 1963. This is another view of the *St Patrick*, showing also the platforms for the railway station and some passenger carriages standing on the railway lines.

Opposite bottom: Weymouth, 2003. This view shows clearly that the dockside station (ferry passenger terminal) has been completely rebuilt since 1963. The new building was opened in May 1980 and while the railway lines are still there, the fact that a car is parked on them might say something about their usage. Part of a ferry's superstructure can be seen to the left of the station.

Right above: Weymouth, 1963. The ship is called the *Roebuck* and is registered at Weymouth. In addition to the ship other forms of transport in this view are, from the left: two small bicycles ridden by little girls, a Rolls-Royce car, a railway goods wagon and a motorbike with sidecar. The presence of the *Roebuck* is consistent with the use of Weymouth as a cargo port.

Right: Weymouth, 1963. This is a view alongside the river looking towards the harbour entrance. It shows the railway line running along the road. Moored on the quayside are both pleasure yachts and fishing boats; indeed a fishing boat is returning to its berth. It is interesting to note the lack of any forms of car parking restrictions.

Above: Weymouth, 1963. Another view of the river looking towards the harbour entrance, this time taken from the Westham bridge. The building on the left is a public house called the Royal Oak, which was clearly owned by the brewer Devenish. Further along the quayside is the Ship Inn, which is in a building dating from the seventeenth century. The moored boats comprise both fishing vessels and pleasure boats. There are many parked cars – several Ford Anglias 105E, a Triumph Herald, an Austin Somerset, an Austin Cambridge and an early Ford Consul. The two other photographs on this page were taken forty years later and show the same stretch of the quay – however, it is immediately apparent that the whole area has been considerably upgraded.

Above right: Weymouth, 2003. Several changes over the past forty years stand out. The George has been renovated and the building to its left has also been given (quite literally) a facelift. The white front of the Ship Inn remains unchanged but the rest of the pub now has a brick facia. The car park has completely disappeared: in its place is a new building with a brick frontage, to integrate with the other buildings. Food has become an increasingly important part of a pub's turnover, and this is clearly shown by two signs outside the Ship Inn – 'bar food' and 'restaurant'. Furthermore, an additional notice says 'Food all day' – this would have been unthinkable in 1963 with the then licensing laws.

Right: Weymouth, 2003. Another view from Westham Bridge, which not only shows the same side of the river but a modern fishing boat as well. A comparison with boats in the 1963 photograph highlights the changes which have occurred in their design. Weymouth continues to have a very active fishing fleet and there are some good fish shops on this quay. There are other signs of the changes of the intervening forty years – the presence of an antiques shop called the 'Curiosity Shoppe' and the restaurant 'Bennett's on the Waterfront'. This is one of several restaurants in this area, and among its offerings is the great British favourite of 'fish and chips'.

Weymouth, 1963. Looking inland from the Westham bridge, the main sights are moored pleasure boats, several cars apparently parked at random, the Sailors Return Inn and finally two large gasometers (gasholders). As well as being concerned with cargo and passenger services, and having a fishing fleet, Weymouth has also been (and still is) a harbour used for recreational boating and sailing.

Right: Weymouth, 2003. This is a direct comparison to the previous photograph and once again shows a number of changes which have occurred over the intermediate forty years. The gasholders have disappeared (presumably as a result of the change from coal gas to natural gas), and a marina has been developed. The front of the inn, and the building to the right, has been changed – most remarkably the door at the side of the pub has disappeared and has been replaced by a window and a continuation of the brick wall.

Next page: Looking across the river to what is now known as Brewer's Quay. This photograph was taken in 1978 and shows the Devenish brewery. This was closed in 1985 after Devenish had been taken over by a pub company. The scene today is more or less unchanged except that many more pleasure boats/yachts are moored on that side. Furthermore, the area around the brewery is now alive with many restaurants.

CHAPTER 4

Portland to Lyme Regis

Previous page: Abbotsbury, 1978. The village of Abbotsbury has long been renowned for its Swannery, but, as a later photograph shows, it is also a charming place. This stretch of the coastline is dominated at first by Chesil Beach, and the Swannery is in a lagoon formed by the beach. The other main feature of this stretch of coast are the fossil-laden cliffs around Lyme Regis and Charmouth.

Left: Pulpit Rock, 1963. The Isle of Portland is some six miles long and it can be a very bleak spot. At the most southerly tip of the Isle is a point known as the Bill of Portland and this has two prominent features: a lighthouse (the current one having been built in 1906) and this feature known as the Pulpit Rock. The symbol painted onto the rock was that used by the Campaign for Nuclear Disarmament (CND). This campaign was most active in the 1950s and 1960s and argued that the UK should unilaterally give up its nuclear weapons.

Below: In the foreground of this 1963 photograph is the town of Wyke Regis, which is almost a suburb of Weymouth. In the distance are the hills on the Isle of Portland and the long strip of land joining them is part of the Chesil Beach (see later). Portland is renowned for two things – Portland stone (used, for example, by Sir Christopher Wren in the construction of St Paul's Cathedral in London) and an ultra-safe harbour, once used by the Royal Navy.

Abbotsbury, 1959. While Abbotsbury is renowned for its Swannery, the centre of the town is a delight.

Charmouth, 1959. In the foreground is an Austin A30. At the time this photograph was taken the road linking Bridport and Honiton, the A35, passed through the centre of this village; nowadays there is a bypass.

This 1963 photograph was taken just outside Abbotsbury on the B3157. In the foreground are two parked cars – an Austin and a Ford Anglia 100E. The building on the hill is St Catherine's chapel, which is the only part of the original monastic buildings in Abbotsbury to remain. It is set on a hill some 250 feet high. In the background are the hills on the Isle of Portland, which stretches away to the right and to the Bill of Portland.

The long strip of land is Chesil Beach, known locally as the eighth wonder of the world, which is seventeen miles long. It is called a barrier beach and is formed of shingle and pebbles, with the individual pieces getting bigger going towards the east. There is a long lagoon between the beach and the mainland proper which is Britain's largest tidal lagoon. As well as being a fine nature reserve it also contains the Swannery, which is believed to be the only managed one of its kind in the world.

Cliffs at Charmouth, 2005. In 2001, this area of the coastline was declared by UNESCO (United Nations Educational, Scientific and Cultural Heritage Organization) to be a World Heritage Site. This is because the exposed cliffs in this area cover a continuous period of some 185 million years. In popular parlance it is known as the 'Jurassic Coast'. For nearly 200 years it has been the site of the discovery of many fossils. In January 2006, there was a major cliff fall in this area, which has exposed many more fossils – to the delight of the palaeontologists.

Right: This street leads from the beach at Lyme Regis (and the car park shown in the photograph below left) into the town centre. It was taken in 1963 and admittedly on a poor day weather-wise, but nevertheless many of the clothes worn by the visitors are very formal, particularly by the standards of the early twenty-first century.

Below: Lyme Regis photographed from the Cobb, 2002. The Cobb is a harbour wall protecting the town from heavy seas and also providing shelter for small boats. In this scene there are both yachts used for recreational sailing and commercial fishing boats.

Lyme Regis, 2002. Lyme Regis is the largest town in the part of the coastline covered in this chapter. It is also very historic, having received its charter in 1285. The use of the word 'Regis' stems from associations with Edward I, who was king from 1272 to 1307. This is one of the main streets, Broad Street, and in the background is the English Channel. It has many fine old buildings, one of which is the Royal Lion hotel. This hotel dates from 1601 and was first opened as a coaching inn.

Lyme Regis, 1963. Taken from a beachside car park, this photograph looks towards Broad Street.

CHAPTER 5

Seaton to Teignmouth

Previous page: Like many other resorts Teignmouth has its own pier, photographed here in 1966. However, while part of it remains, a recent visit (March 2006) has confirmed that the buildings at the end of the pier are no longer there.

Left above: Sidmouth, 1963. Geographically, Sidmouth is a few miles along the coast from Seaton, on the way to Exmouth and hence eventually to Teignmouth. However, like Lyme Regis, its development occurred well before the coming of the railways: it is the oldest of the resorts along this stretch of coast and has lovely Georgian and Regency houses on its sea front. The most distinctive features in this photograph are the lamp-post in the middle of the photograph and the people walking along the promenade. Like many previous shots, the people are wearing very formal clothes.

Left: Seaton, 1963. This is a small seaside resort in Devon, and it is interesting to see fishing boats standing on the beach. Seaton, Sidmouth and Lyme Regis all have one thing in common and that is that they lie in gaps between high cliffs.

Beer, 2002. Close to Seaton is the small fishing port of Beer. It has no natural harbour and so the boats are hauled onto the beach. The boat on the right hand side is offering the chance to go mackerel fishing to anyone visiting Beer. As befits a small fishing village, there are very good fish shops near the front.

Above left: Teignmouth, taken from Shaldon, 1957. Although tourism is now one of its main industries, Teignmouth has a long history and was at one time a major fishing port and shipbuilding centre. The river Teign rises in Dartmoor and reaches the sea at this point.

Above: Taken in 1968, the small boat in the middle of the river with people aboard is the passenger ferry from Teignmouth to Shaldon. This view is from Shaldon looking across to Teignmouth.

Left: The Ness, 1957. The Ness is a large dark red sandstone headland, and this view of it, looking across the Teign estuary towards Torquay, was taken from Teignmouth.

CHAPTER 6

Torquay

Previous page: Torquay, 1966. Although they may nest some distance away, herring gulls still manage to find their way to Torquay as the 'pickings' (bread or other food thrown by holidaymakers) can be quite substantial.

Above: Torquay, 1968. Taken from the harbour wall, this view looks towards one area of the town. While Torquay had been a fishing village for some time, it was the coming of the railway in the 1840s that allowed the townspeople to transform it into a leading seaside resort. They did this by publicising the fact that Torquay had a relatively mild climate (by English standards). The whole region of Torbay (Torquay, Brixham and Paignton) was marketed as the 'English Riviera' and Torquay was proclaimed to be its 'Queen'. There are many buildings in Torquay dating from Victorian and Edwardian times. It is now one of the largest resorts in England. Despite the downturn in the traditional fortnight's holiday, Torquay has nevertheless continued to attract visitors by various well-directed programmes.

Right: Torquay, 2006. What an astounding change! While the buildings in the distance are more or less the same, a part of the harbour has now become one gigantic marina.

Above: Torquay, 1968. This is another view looking towards the centre of town from the harbour wall.

Left: Torquay, 2006. This view shows that in addition to the marina there has been yet another change in the harbour. In the 1968 view the Pavilion, constructed in 1912, is clearly visible on the left hand side of the above picture, but this is no longer the case. Instead, there is now a new pier, with many large buildings, jutting out into the centre of the harbour. The other change is the number of new buildings which are on the upper parts of the hill immediately behind the church.

This crowded Torquay beach scene was photographed in 1966. While people are wearing a wide range of different fashions, the overall effect is one of less formality than the scenes from Weymouth in 1963. This is particularly true of the younger people, and may even be a reflection of the fact that 1966 was one of the central years of the 'Swinging Sixties'.

Clockwise from top left:

Torquay, 1966. Taken in the summer, these young men are clearly in a jaunty holiday mood; and never a baseball cap in sight!

Torquay, 1966. These people are standing near a kiosk selling newspapers and magazines. This photograph was taken in mid-summer, but not everyone was wearing casual clothes.

Torquay, 1966. These people are walking along the harbour wall. This has been printed to give a deliberately graphic approach. However, once again, note those fashions.

Torquay railway station, 1966. While many people travelled to Torquay (and other places) by car, the trains were still a much-used form of transport. This scene shows people, with their suitcases, waiting to catch a train going in the London direction. Again it is the fashions which are so different from today, as all look smartly dressed – every man is wearing a jacket, some have ties, several women are wearing hats and there is a boy with tailored shorts and long socks.

CHAPTER 7

Brixham

Previous page: Brixham, 1957. Brixham has always been an important fishing centre, and today it is possibly the second most important one in the South West after Newlyn (which is not featured in this book). It was Brixham's fishermen who, in the eighteenth century, developed the skill of using trawl nets for catching fish. When these photographs were taken the old harbour was still very much at the centre of landing the catch, but this is no longer the case as a new fish quay was opened in 1990. Hence, the next sequence of photographs records a way of life that has changed significantly. The harbour is surrounded by hills with fishermen's cottages, many dating from the Victorian period.

Left above: Resulting from its close proximity to both Torquay and Paignton, Brixham received many visitors attracted by its fishing harbour. Among those visitors were my parents, and this photograph was taken by my father in the middle to latter part of the 1930s. Brixham's port has a fine and long history. One intriguing fact is that it is the only place in Britain visited by Napoleon: this was shortly after the battle of Waterloo, when he was brought here to change ships en route to St Helena and exile. There is also a statue to William of Orange, who landed here in November 1688 and subsequently became William III.

Left below: Photographed in 2006, this updates the view taken in the 1930s. There is little physical change in the buildings fronting onto the harbour, but inevitably there are changes in their use reflecting the greater importance of tourism. The style and design of the yachts and boats in the harbour is now, seventy years later, very different. However, the real change is further into town, with the disappearance of the gasometer, and maybe the reconstruction of some of the buildings.

Below: Brixham, 1957. Although taken from the opposite side of the harbour, this photograph does overlap with the other two on this page. The gasometer is still there, and where the overlap occurs it can easily be seen that the buildings have not changed in the period between the 1930s and 1957. It is possible to read some of the shop names on a big print; one which stands out clearly is H.C. Wood, chemist. Other buildings house a ship's chandler, engineers, an ironmonger and finally a pub called Buller's Arms. The foreground is netting on one of the fishing boats.

Brixham 1968. A fishing boat is just arriving, the entrance from the sea being just beyond it. From a photographer's point of view, fishing harbours are always fascinating as usually so much is happening.

Brixham, 1968. Here a fisherman is working on his catch while herring gulls fly about, scrounging whatever scraps they can find.

Brixham, 1957. And always, in the background, or in the foreground, are the gulls, mainly herring gulls. The dark bird on the left has the plumage of a young bird and is making itself heard. One of the great delights of so many British seaside resorts and fishing harbours is the sound of the gulls. In the South West, it is the herring gull which seems to be the most prevalent.

Brixham, 1966. The design of cars is one factor that dates photographs more quickly than many others. At the time this photograph was taken, most cars on the road were produced in Britain, and among the makes to be seen here are: Ford, Austin, Morris, Rover, Wolseley and Sunbeam. Ford seems to be the most popular make. In the background there is a couple with a young child in a pushchair; it comes as a shock to realise that this child is now over forty years of age!

Opposite: Brixham 1968. On the far bank are some more of the cottages plus some other buildings which were no doubt connected to the fishing industry. The waterside stone buildings have been refaced and renewed and now house HM Coastguard. The chimney has been demolished and in its place is a large building with many apartments.

Right: Brixham, 1966.

Below: Brixham, 1966. Brixham is not only a photographer's delight, but one that attracts artists as well. There is so much to see and record.

Left top: In addition to cars, fashions also date photographs. Here is a group of holidaymakers in Brixham in 1966 enjoying the sun, with a range of clothes that were popular then. As noted elsewhere in this book, in the early and mid 1960s, these were often quite formal; for instance, men with ties and jackets.

Left middle: Brixham Carnival in the 1930s; these two photographs were taken by my mother. For me, the remarkable aspect of both of them is the clothes. On the left is a young woman with a white pinafore – is she a waitress in a local café or was she 'in service'? Furthermore, the policeman on the right is standing strictly to attention.

Left bottom: Another shot taken during the Carnival. So many things to observe: the haircuts of the young boys; maybe it was a chilly day, but the women are wearing overcoats, and most remarkably, hats.

Below: Could there be a more complete contrast to the two previous photographs? Seventy years on and Brixham now houses a marina with a large number of ocean-going yachts for recreational sailing – reflecting both changing lifestyles and today's much higher incomes. The marina is housed in the outer harbour – this photograph being taken from the wall of the outer harbour. Beyond the marina, two modern fishing vessels can be seen moored beside the new fish quay.

CHAPTER 8

Dartmouth to Plymouth

Previous page: The river Dart, at Dartmouth, 1966. The river Dart is one of the main rivers of South Devon. Its headwaters are on Dartmoor where two branches, the East Dart and West Dart, join at Dartmeet. It then flows past Buckfastleigh (site of Buckfast Abbey) and Totnes to reach the open sea at Dartmouth. This photograph shows the view looking up the river Dart towards Totnes.

Left: Dartmouth, 1966. The town of Dartmouth has some interesting old corners. Bearing in mind that it is set among hills it will come as no surprise to find a steep stepped lane such as this. As well as being a holiday and yachting resort, Dartmouth is also famous for its Royal Naval College.

Below: The centre of Dartmouth lies in a valley on the western side of the river, which can be seen in the distance in this 1957 photograph. The town has a very long maritime history going well back into the Middle Ages.

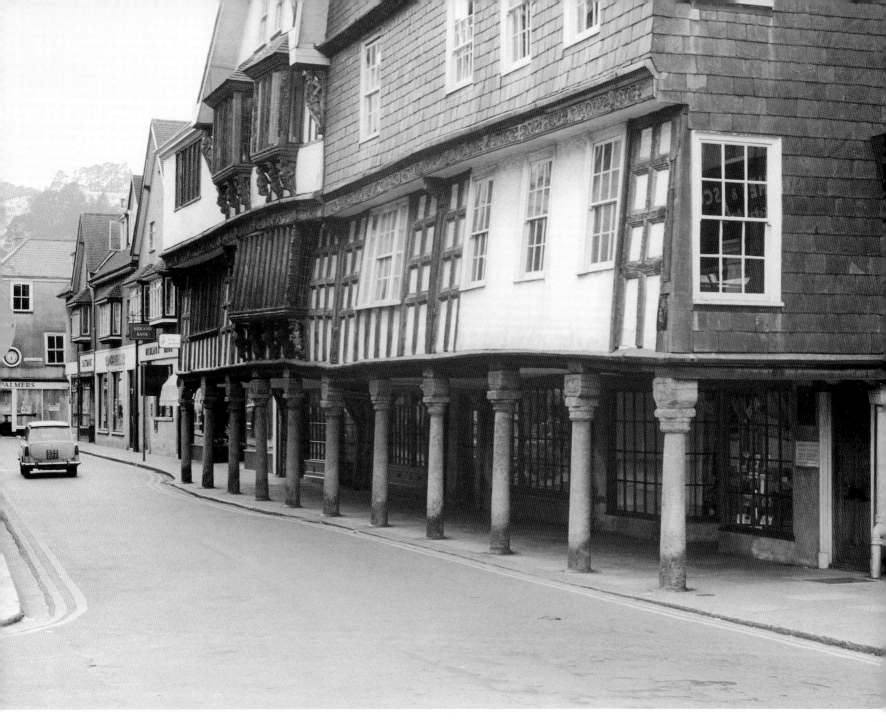

Dartmouth, 1966. Parking is restricted by the double yellow lines – a relatively recent innovation. The key feature is the Butterwalk, which is the group of shops overhanging the pavement. The shops were built between 1635 and 1640 and the overhangs are supported by eleven granite pillars.

Slapton Sands, 1966. Although in the middle of summer, and while Torquay was packed, there are very few people on the beach at Slapton. An obvious reason why the beach is so deserted is that there were no beach cafés and toilets along the whole stretch of this beach. At the time when I was there, there was no monument to the large number of American troops that had been killed prior to D-Day in 1944. Slapton Sands are located in Start Bay.

Salcombe, 1966. Salcombe is situated on the Kingsbridge Estuary, and while many of the inlets have small fishing communities, Salcombe is very much a centre for leisure sailing.

Taken in 1966, this is one of the many narrow streets leading from Salcombe harbour. A yachtsman, or fisherman, is returning home at the end of the day. Salcombe is the most southerly resort in Devon.

Hope Cove, 1966. There are many small bays and coves along this stretch of coastline. The area between Dartmouth and almost to Plymouth is known as the South Hams (Ham is an old English word meaning shelter) and claims to have the most mild climate in England.

Noss Mayo, 2002. There is a large inlet off the coast called the Yealm estuary, where small yachting and holiday communities flourish. Noss Mayo is one of these, and on another part of this inlet is Newton Ferrers. This wooded and serene inlet is only a few miles away from the large urban area of Plymouth.

CHAPTER 9

Plymouth

Previous page: Plymouth Hoe, 1955. In 1759 this lighthouse had been built by John Smeaton on Eddystone Reef. The Eddystone Reef is some fifteen miles from the Hoe and has always been very dangerous to shipping. It was for this reason that a lighthouse was first placed on the reef in 1698. However, this original building and its immediate successor did not survive for very long, and so Smeaton designed a granite lighthouse which entered service about 1760. However, even this building eventually became unsafe and was taken down and replaced by yet another tower. The top part of Smeaton's lighthouse was then transferred to the Hoe and opened to the general public in 1884 as a memorial to the architect. It is now known as Smeaton's Tower.

Plymouth, 2006. The most striking change since 1955 has been the construction of a block of flats, partially on the site where there were tennis courts. It was not possible to get precisely the same viewpoint as in 1955 because of the growth of trees on the side of the Hoe.

Plymouth, photographed from the Hoe in 1955. Plymouth has a long and distinguished history and is one of the largest towns featured in this book. Plymouth was already an important commercial port by the Middle Ages and has links with many famous sea-going explorers such as Sir Francis Drake and Captain Cook. It was from here that the *Mayflower* left for America in 1620. However, it began its journey at Rotherhithe in London and there is a reference to this in my first book *London's River*. Plymouth became a major port for the Royal Navy at the end of the seventeenth century. As already noted, William of Orange, subsequently William III (1689-1702), landed at nearby Brixham and it was in his reign that the first contracts to construct the docks were awarded. The docks were in Devonport but this town was incorporated into Plymouth in 1914.

Right: This view was taken by my mother in the 1930s from the Hoe, from almost identically the same spot as my 1955 and 2006 photographs. Despite the very heavy destruction of the centre of Plymouth by the 'Blitz' in 1941 a comparison between the two photographs show that some of the houses still remained in 1955. However, the most striking building, the pier, had disappeared. It was built in 1884 and destroyed during the Blitz.

Plymouth, 1968. Another view taken from the Hoe: this shows the same small harbour which has featured in the previous photographs. The island in the centre is called 'Drake's Island'. To the left of the Island, and just visible on the horizon, is a breakwater and the space between that structure, the island and the surrounding land is called Plymouth Sound. To the right of the island is a stretch of water which leads to the docks and to the river Tamar. The breakwater was designed by John Rennie and work began in 1812, and for many years limestone blocks were put into the sea – in the end totalling some 4 or 5 million tons of stone. This same man – John Rennie – is referred to several times in my book *London's River*, as he designed several bridges across the Thames including the 1831 London Bridge. The main change by 2006 was the construction of a block of flats on the site of the open land.

Plymouth, 1966. Again taken from the Hoe, this is a close-up of some of the buildings seen earlier in this chapter (obtained by using a telephoto lens).

Plymouth, 1966. Another close-up of these buildings showing cars of the period, which are nearly all UK produced. Intriguingly, there is a washing line hanging between the rear walls of two of the houses. The tennis courts and open land have been replaced by a block of flats and gardens.

Right: This photograph was taken by my mother from Smeaton's Tower on the Hoe in the 1930s. The central tall pillar is the Naval War Memorial. This 100 foot column records the names of 22,443 men killed in the two world wars and was designed by Sir Richard Lorimer. The tower to the right is the National Armada Memorial, and is shown in more detail in the image below.

This was the scene a few years before virtually the whole of the city centre was obliterated by the five day Blitz in 1941. In this view there are a few spires and towers which stand out above the generality of the house tops, and these are:

• On the far left is the spire of the Roman Catholic cathedral.

• The tall tower reaching out above the horizon to the right of the Naval Memorial is the municipal building

• Nearby is the wide roofed building with a narrow spire which is the Guildhall, built around 1800.

• Then to the far right, with a tower appearing just above the trees, is the 136 feet high tower of St Andrew's church. There has been a church on this site since Norman times, although the one shown here dates from the fifteenth century.

Most of these buildings were destroyed by the Blitz, but the Guildhall and parts of St Andrew's church (including the tower) survived. The church was subsequently rebuilt and then re-consecrated in 1957.

Right: Plymouth, 2006. The National Armada Memorial can be clearly seen in this photograph with the figure of Britannia atop its tower. Changes in the skyline are immediately obvious.

Far right: Plymouth, 2006. This is another view of Plymouth's new skyline. Between the tree and the square building on the right (a hotel) is a tall tower. This is attached to the Guildhall.

Plymouth, 1966. There are some fine old houses by the Hoe, and I spotted this man wearing a tuxedo looking from one of the windows of these houses.

Drake's statue on Plymouth Hoe, 1955. The statue was formally unveiled to the public in 1884 by a descendant of Sir Francis Drake and is the work of Sir Edgar Boehm. The modern looking building behind it was not there in the 1930s and it had disappeared by 2006, to be replaced by trees. Drake sailed from Plymouth on several occasions, including 1577 when he commenced the journey which led eventually to him and his crew making the first journey around the world.

Plymouth, 1966. These two Royal Navy ships are in the Sound, with the Cornish coastline in the distance.

Plymouth, 1966. This view is looking towards Drake's Island and the Cornish side of the Sound.

Plymouth, 1966. This is taken from further round the coast, and shows (at the bottom) the Ferry Boat Inn. The name of this public house is clearly derived from the fact that there were two ferries linking Plymouth with towns on the Cornish bank of the Sound.

Plymouth, 1957. This photograph is a reminder that although the city was a major Royal Navy port, it was also used by trans-Atlantic liners.

The river Tamar is the boundary between Devon and Cornwall, and is crossed near Plymouth by these two bridges. The Great Western Railway Co. was the one which served this part of the country, and the bridge on the left was built when the GWR extended its routes into Cornwall. Called the Royal Albert Bridge, it was designed and built by Isambard Kingdom Brunel in 1857-59. Brunel was one of the truly great Victorian engineers. The bridge on the right is the Tamar Road Bridge. Opened in 1962, it replaced the Saltash ferry. This photograph was taken in 1966.

The size of the boat passing underneath gives some idea of the size of the granite piers which support Brunel's Bridge. The buildings on the far bank are in Saltash in Cornwall. The river flows from right to left, descending from Tavistock towards Plymouth Sound and the sea. This photograph was taken in 1966.

Previous page: Two of the Biodomes at the Eden project, photographed in 2004. The Eden Project has been one of the most commercially successful of the Millennium projects in the UK, and more details appear later in this chapter. This part of the South Cornish coast is an amalgam of fishing villages, holiday resorts, beautiful gardens and old industrial areas.

Left above: This view of Looe was taken by my father in the later 1930s. After leaving Plymouth and crossing into Cornwall, Looe is the first of what may be described as the 'well known' old fishing villages. The bridge over the river Looe is Victorian and links East and West Looe.

Left below: This is Polperro, and this view, also taken in the later 1930s, shows the entrance to Polperro harbour. Looe is often associated with Polperro, which is the next fishing village along the coast, albeit the two of them are very different.

Opposite, clockwise from top left:
Polperro Harbour, 1957. Polperro has a very picturesque harbour at the base of steep hills and boasts a museum on smuggling. In preparing the captions for this book, I found the word 'smuggling' mentioned against many of the places on the South West coast.

Polperro Harbour, 1957.

One feature of Polperro is its narrow lanes and whitewashed stone houses, as featured in this photograph taken in the later 1930s.

Polruan, 1957. Further along the coast is Polruan, a small village on the opposite bank to Fowey, from where this photograph was taken. While Fowey is a commercial port, Polruan is concerned with recreational sailing and yachting.

Top left: Fowey, 1957. As well as being a bustling holiday resort, Fowey has had for centuries a busy commercial harbour and is a major port for the export of china clay. The river is also called the Fowey, and is one of the many sheltered inlets on the south Cornish coast.

Above: Fowey, 1957. The cargo boat shown here is called the *Spaarnestroom* and is of Dutch origin. It appears from a specialist web-site that there have been at least three ships with this name, the first operating in the period 1920-1928 and the third working from 1964. The middle one, presumably this vessel, was constructed in 1947 and presumably ceased operating (under this name at least) by the early 1960s.

Top right: In 1978, I played golf at the (then) newly established course at Carlyon Bay. This course is beside the sea, but what was unexpected were the smoking chimneys and the adjacent factory.

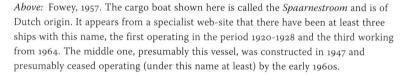

Opposite middle right: Although Cornwall is nowadays a major holiday destination, it has a very long industrial history. One of those industries is the quarrying of china clay and these pits were photographed near St Austell in 1962.

Opposite bottom right: This is another view of some of the china clay pits near St Austell, photographed in 1962. China clay is in effect decomposed granite and the industry developed after the discovery of this clay by William Cookworthy around 1750. The disused buildings are another part of the industry and the landscape. It is necessary to dry the clay and these buildings were 'pan kilns' which were introduced in the 1850s. Up to then the clay had been dried naturally; nowadays the pan kilns have been superseded by a different technique.

Above: Eden Project, 2004. This was built as a Millennium project and opened to the public in March 2001. It has become the leading tourist destination in the South West with 1.2 million visitors per year, and employs some 500 people. It was built in a disused china clay quarry, like the ones shown in the two photographs on the opposite page. The quarry is some fifty metres deep and the site covers a total area of fifty hectares. The large buildings are called Biomes – one biome houses plants from the humid tropics while the second is concerned with warm temperate areas. The Eden Project is owned by an educational charitable trust and its aim is the study of the plant world and to demonstrate its importance in everyday life.

Opposite: The 'Lost Gardens' of Heligan are now one of Cornwall's major tourist attractions, and how this has come about is truly an amazing story. The gardens originally reached their peak in 1914 and then subsequently deteriorated. They were found again after the 1990 hurricane and have been reclaimed: today the project employs some 100 people. Indeed some of the areas had been completely overgrown and it was only after much hard work that the original plants were uncovered. Photographed in 2004, this tree fern, which is a plant native to Australia and New Zealand, is in part of the gardens called 'The Jungle', which is a long, deep valley sheltered enough to have many different tropical and sub-tropical plants.

Right: Mevagissey is another small fishing village full of narrow streets and buildings dating back many decades. Photographed here in 1966, it is also a very popular tourist destination.

Mevagissey, 2004. The only noticeable change over the past four decades is in the design of the small boats.

Left: Mevagissey, 1966. There are some other changes which are highlighted by a comparison between this photograph and the next one.

Right: Restaurants in Mevagissey, 2004. Over the thirty-eight years, the buildings have been upgraded, with new fronts. Over this time span eating out has become increasingly popular and diners have come to expect a much higher standard of service and range and quality of food on the menu. Hence the really noticeable change in the type of café is not surprising: instead of a simple 'fish and chip' shop, there is now a 'Mr Bistro' seafood restaurant. The Shark's Fin restaurant is in both photographs and a comparison shows how it has become larger and its front been redesigned. Furthermore, in 1968 cafés had only just started to take advantage of the new restaurant licence, but by 2004 it is certain that these outlets would be selling alcoholic drinks, especially wine.

St Mawes castle, 2004. This town has a very mild climate and is a holiday and yachting centre. Its castle stands opposite the one at Falmouth, and they were built by Henry VIII (who reigned from 1509 to 1547) to protect the Carrick Roads (yet another big inlet from the sea) from foreign invasion. The view beyond the castle is towards the open sea.

Above: This couple, and their dog, are clearly enjoying a rest, and the summer sunshine, in St Mawes in 1978.

Above: This pub was photographed in 1978, and it still existed in 2004. It is one of the many pubs in Cornish fishing harbours which have a nautical theme in their name. This pub was operated by the brewer Devenish, which in 1978 had two breweries: in Weymouth (see chapter 3) and Redruth, an industrial town in Cornwall. Some years after this shot was taken Devenish was bought by a pub company and its Weymouth brewery closed (and converted into a pub) while its Redruth brewery continued in production until 2004, albeit under the ownership of several different operators.

Left: The Carrick Roads are crossed by a small chain ferry called the *King Harry Ferry*. There are usually several ships moored upriver – not needed, not in use and, to use a phrase, laid up 'in mothballs'. This view, dating from 1985, was taken in an autumnal mist.

CHAPTER 11

From the Fal to Land's End

Previous page: The stretch of Cornish coastal scenery covered by this chapter is full of small fishing harbours, such as Mullion shown in this 2004 photograph. It is remarkable how narrow the entrance to Mullion's harbour is. However, there are also some other fine sights, such as Pendennis Castle and St Michael's Mount.

The battlements of Pendennis castle, Falmouth, 1967. This castle was built at the same time as the one in St Mawes, the reason being to defend the entrance to Carrick Roads, which is a fine deep water harbour.

Coverack, 2004. This is one of the many small fishing villages dotted around the Cornish coast. In times past it was also used for smuggling – perhaps the most popular of the smuggled goods being spirits.

In the foreground of this 1967 photograph are some of the buildings of Pendennis castle, while beyond it is the town of Falmouth. Falmouth's early development was as a port, and indeed it is still the largest one in Cornwall, but with the coming of the railways it also became an important holiday and sailing centre.

Coverack, 2004. A sign of the times has reached this small community. The old lifeboat house has been converted into a café and bistro, once again reflecting the trend towards eating out.

Top: Cadgwith, 2004. This is another very small Cornish fishing village; the letters on the front of the fishing boats are the registration number and FH refers to Falmouth.

Above: The 'earth station' at Goonhilly Down shortly after it became operational, 1962. Since taking this photograph the site has grown tremendously and is central to much telecommunications work. It sends, and receives, messages via specialised satellites. It was near here (Poldhu) in December 1901 that Marconi's wireless station received transatlantic radio signals for the first time.

Right: Taken from Lizard Point in 2004, this view is looking westwards. In the base, at sea level, is the building housing the Lizard lifeboat. The headland is some 186 feet above the sea.

Cafés and other buildings on Lizard Point, 2004. The Lizard is the most southerly point on the English mainland.

Mullion is one of the prettiest harbours on the Cornish coast and is, perhaps uniquely, owned by the National Trust. Autumnal sea mists are not unusual on the Cornish coast, and this photograph, taken in 1985, shows the harbour in one such mist. The first photograph in this chapter shows the narrow entrance to the harbour, and the following two photographs show other aspects of it.

Mullion harbour, 2004. This view shows two of the small fishing boats which still operate from this harbour, albeit tourism is probably a more important source of income for this community. The letters PZ in the registration number relate to Penzance.

This photograph was taken in 2004 showing a cottage or store right on the harbour-side. In the foreground are some lobster pots. As well as looking after the harbour walls, the National Trust is also responsible for maintaining some of the small buildings located around the harbour.

Opposite: St Michael's Mount, 1985. One way of reaching the island is by a causeway, which can be seen on the left of this photograph. The island has a long history, featuring in many Cornish myths. The current structure at the top of the hill dates from the latter part of the seventeenth century and is a house/castle with a church. It is quite different from St Michael's Mount in Brittany, which is bigger and higher, with shops and cafés at the base and an abbey at the top.

Also photographed in 1967, these lovely slabs are on the quayside at the harbour on St Michael's Mount. They stand out well due to the intense and low angle sunlight of early autumn.

However, when the tide is in the island can only be reached by a ferry, such as this one crossing to St Michael's Mount in 1967.

The small harbour on the island of St Michael's Mount, 1967. The harbour and causeway were rebuilt just before 1730.

One of the small shops by the harbour can be seen in this 1967 photograph. The Cornish mainland can be seen in the distance.

A final view of St Michael's Mount, 1967, now owned by the National Trust. In the foreground is one of the small passenger ferries which take visitors over to the island, along with two of the boatmen.

Above: Mousehole, 1967. The origins of its name are uncertain with more than one suggestion being put forward; what is not in dispute is its pronunciation – 'mouzzel'. It is one of the most ancient of the Cornish ports and suffered a raid by Spanish privateers in 1595 – after which only one building remained. Mousehole was not alone in suffering from such an invasion. Between them, the French and the Spaniards invaded Fowey in 1457, Marazion in 1514, Newlyn and Penzance in 1595. Mousehole is another small fishing port, and at one time its fishermen were actively engaged in fishing for pilchards. Nowadays, there are likely to be as many recreational sailing boats moored in the harbour as there are fishing boats. One interesting feature to emerge from this 1967 photograph is the smoke coming from various chimneys, presumably from coal fires. In December 1981, there was a terrible lifeboat disaster. The Penlee lifeboat vessel *Solomon Browne* was lost and eight Mousehole men died – this occurred while trying to rescue the crew of the *Union Star*. The event is remembered by a plaque on the outside wall of a Mousehole pub.

Left: Land's End, 1957. As a photographer I have always liked photographing the sun *contre jour* (against the light) on water. Here the lighting emphasises the rocks of the coast as well as the 123 feet high Longships lighthouse. This is just one of many lighthouses in this part of Cornwall, based either on land or on rocks out at sea, established to help protect shipping from rocky outcrops such as these. There is a finality about the name 'Land's End', which is indeed the most westerly point in England.

CHAPTER 12

St Ives and nearby

Previous page: Perranporth, 1967. Perranporth was once a mining community, but with the coming of the railways it developed into a holiday resort utilising its fine beaches. However, the reason for its inclusion in this book is its fine rock formations which are clearly the result of erosion by the sea and wind.

Left top: St Ives, 2004. St Ives is on the north Cornish coast which is quite different from that to the south of the county. The north coast is on the Atlantic seaboard whereas the south coast is sheltered from the Atlantic storms, has much larger inlets and is therefore more sheltered and warmer. Furthermore, the south coast's many large inlets provide natural harbours, but such safe havens are much fewer (and often far between) on the north coast.

　　The first communities living in St Ives were concerned for many centuries with fishing, and fishing vessels still sail from the harbour. While commercial fishing still continues, it is quite likely that many of the fishing trips occur when the boats are hired by holidaymakers. On the far side of the harbour is the church of St Ia, named after an Irish missionary. This church was built in the early part of the fifteenth century.

Left bottom: St. Ives, 1967. St Ives is the biggest town covered in this chapter. This picture shows one of the main streets, called the Wharf, which runs alongside the harbour and moored boats. It is full of shops, restaurants and pubs, but not surprisingly there have been changes since 1967.

Opposite top left: Porthminster beach, St Ives, 1967. There are three different facets to St Ives. One of these is as a thriving holiday centre, with plenty of beaches – this one is on the northern side of the town.

Opposite top right: Tate, St Ives, 2004. As well as being a holiday centre and fishing community, St Ives third claim to fame is as an art centre. This aspect of St Ives started in the 1880s when several nationally known artists came to live in the town, and they were subsequently followed in the twentieth century by many others. The most recent addition to St Ives' notable buildings is shown in this photograph – the Tate Gallery. The gallery is located on the site of an old gasworks and building work began in June 1991: and it was formally opened by HRH Prince Charles on 23 June 1993. It stands opposite Portmeor beach. (While this gallery is sited on an old gasworks, the Tate Modern Gallery is housed in an old electrical power generating station beside the Thames in London.)

Above: A one-man band photographed in St Ives in 1978. Clothing fashions change over time, but then so do hairstyles.

Right: One of the delights of St Ives is the many side streets and lanes, such as this one photographed in 1967. However, one of the changes since 1967 is the greater number of these streets where the houses are brightly painted, many being shops selling tourist souvenirs and art galleries.

Photographed in 1985, this is part of the Levant tin mine, near Pendeen, which is between Land's End and St Ives. Nowadays the mine is owned by the National Trust and open to the public. The Levant mine closed in 1930 and was one of those where the tunnels went out under the sea. It was the advent of the steam engine which made it possible for the mines to go ever deeper as the machines facilitated water drainage.

For many centuries, Cornwall was one of the world's most important tin mining centres; indeed some of the records go back at least 2,000 years. The fortunes of Cornish mines started to change in the middle of the nineteenth century due to competition from producers in other parts of the world and a downturn in the world price of tin. Continued fluctuations in this price meant that mines would re-open and then close again. Nowadays, the mines are closed (although sometimes one or two re-open depending upon the world price for tin) and there are signs everywhere of disused mines. While much emphasis is given to tin, Cornwall was also a source of other raw materials, such as copper.

CHAPTER 13

Newquay to Boscastle

Previous page: This photograph of Fistral Beach was taken in the evening sunlight on a spring day in 2004. This is one of England's premier surfing beaches, and the Atlantic rollers are shown as shadows in the *contre jour* lighting.

Left: Crantock beach is south of Newquay, between Pentire Points East and West, and this photograph of it was taken in 1967. The emptiness of the scene has a magic, particularly in the low angle sunlight of autumn which emphases the footprints on the beach.

Below: Fistral beach, 2004. In the foreground someone is carrying a surfboard towards the sea. The north Cornish coast takes on a new dimension, as there are many beaches along this part of the coast where the Atlantic Ocean provides the kind of sea which is a surfer's delight.

Above: Taken in 1967, this view of Fistral Beach is looking north towards Newquay, and the large building standing out on the headland is the Headland Hotel. The popularity of surfing as a sport has increased significantly since this view was taken and this in turn has led to the construction of a large group of buildings at the far end of the beach meeting the various needs of surfers.

Right: Newquay harbour, 2004. The name 'Newquay' derives from the construction of a new quay to protect the harbour in 1439. It was for many centuries a fishing port and then it also became a commercial port for a few years in the nineteenth century. However, as with many other towns included within this book, Newquay changed radically with the coming of the railways. Quite simply it became a holiday destination and is now the biggest resort on the north Cornish coast. Nevertheless, as can be seen here, there are still some small fishing boats which sail from this harbour.

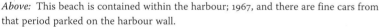

Above: This beach is contained within the harbour; 1967, and there are fine cars from that period parked on the harbour wall.

Top right: Newquay, 1967. This beach, Towan, is situated just north of the harbour and has a small promenade beside it. This photograph was taken during the autumn and so many of the small kiosks on the prom are closed but there is a van parked there selling Wall's Ice Cream. At the top of the cliffs are some of the houses and hotels built at the time when Newquay was developing as a holiday resort.

Bottom right: Newquay, 1967. However, it is not unknown to have poor weather, and these people are sitting under cover, well wrapped up to keep warm. Furthermore, they are outside 'Cosy Nook Theatre', and there are posters proclaiming that 'This evening at 8.30 it is Showtime'. This kind of entertainment is typical of English seaside resorts. The cars are a Hillman Imp and an Armstrong Siddeley. (There were also some fine sunny days when people sat in the open sunning themselves and drinking at bars etc.)

Opposite: Newquay, 1967. This photograph is taken from a cave in the cliffs which surround the beaches north of the harbour. It is looking back towards the town. Note the fashions.

Left: Looking north along the coast towards Bedruthan Steps, this 1967 photograph shows some of the fine beaches north of Newquay, such as Great Western and Tolcarne.

Opposite: Bedruthan Steps, 1967. This is another superb spot on the north Cornish coast; on this particular day the waves and surf of the North Atlantic look spectacular. The rocky nature of the beach results in the main from the effects of the Atlantic Ocean. The name is associated with a mythical giant called Bedruthan; this sector of the coastline is owned by the National Trust.

Below: Most photographs are taken in good weather, but equally stunning coastal scenery is on hand when the weather is stormy; as shown here in this 1962 photograph. This particular viewpoint is a few miles north of Bedruthan Steps.

Top left: Part of Boscastle harbour, 1967. Boscastle is sited in a narrow combe and fed by three different rivers. In August 2004, there was a sudden, torrential downpour, and within a couple of hours Boscastle was the scene of some terrible floods. Thankfully no one was killed but many people had to be rescued by helicopters.

Top right: Moored boats within Boscastle harbour in 1967; a fisherman is preparing one of the boats for departure (this is PW243 which appears in the next picture). Part of the harbour piers date from the sixteenth century.

Left: The final photograph in this sequence, taken in 1967, shows the small boat approaching the open sea. The entrance to Boscastle harbour is between these huge 300 feet cliffs, and the small boat is dwarfed by them. It is nearing sunset, and once again I was photographically attracted to the effect of the sunlight shining on water.

Previoous page: Clovelly, 1957. There is one link between Clovelly, Boscastle and Ilfracombe, and this is that these three places are among the only ones with a safe harbour in this stretch of the English coast. Clovelly is one of the South West coast's 'showpiece' villages, famous for its steeply cobbled hill. This view of the village is taken from the harbour wall, which was built in the sixteenth century.

Left: Clovelly is the village nearest to Cornwall on the North Devon coast. This 1964 picture, taken at the top of the hill, shows the steep cobbled path which leads down through the village to the harbour. The walk from here to the harbour is about half a mile and the descent is some 400 feet. It is cobbled all the way and visitors' motor cars and coaches have to be parked at the top of the hill. The cottages also date from the sixteenth century.

Opposite, top left: This view of Ilfracombe harbour was photographed in 1964 from one of the hills which surround the town. It is a natural harbour and able to protect various kinds of boats from the ravages of Atlantic storms. It is also one of the few natural harbours along the north coast of Devon. The buildings around the harbour include shops, restaurants and a pub.

Opposite, bottom left: Like many such communities around our coast, Ilfracombe has its own lifeboat and this 1957 photograph shows the lifeboat being taken from its shed by tractor towards its slipway at the end of the harbour. This was a time-consuming process and it took some ten minutes for the lifeboat to be towed from its housing through a couple of streets to the harbour. A new boathouse, very close to its harbour slipway, was opened in May 1996.

Opposite, top right: Ilfracombe, 2006. Since the opening of the new lifeboat boathouse, the old boathouse has been converted into an aquarium.

Opposite, bottom right: Ilfracombe, 1957. Now launched, the lifeboat is seen here setting out to sea. My impression at the time was that this was a training run rather than an actual emergency as everyone seemed so relaxed.

This book has covered two obvious aspects of sea safety – one is the need for lighthouses and the other the need for lifeboats. Records show that Ilfracombe's first lifeboat came into service in 1828, while the vessel shown here is the *Robert and Phemia Brown*. This particular lifeboat was known as a Liverpool type and entered service in 1953, being replaced in 1966. During this period of time it was launched to meet emergencies on forty-six different occasions, saving twenty-four lives.

Opposite: Ilfracombe harbour, 1957. This view is looking towards the centre of the town and the striped spire of the church can be seen above the harbour side buildings. The road to the right is very busy with plenty of people and cars – the only one which can be easily discerned is an Austin A30.

At the far end of the harbour is the Royal Britannia Hotel, which is shown as being owned by Georges' brewery. By 1970 Georges' brewery was no more and its plant and pubs had become part of the Courage operation.

Right: Ilfracombe, 2006. There is little change in the harbour side buildings over the past four decades.

Below: Ilfracombe, 2006. This is another view of the harbour, showing the slipway used by the lifeboat, with its new boathouse perfectly situated at the top of the slipway.

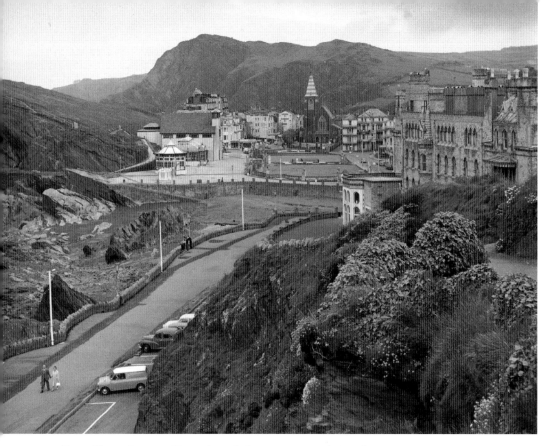

A final thought

The changes inferred from the final pair of photographs and other images taken over a fifty year period shown in this book are consistent with the changes shown in my other books: *London's River* and *Essex Thames-side*. Over this period of five decades there have been momentous developments, such as the introduction of the World Wide Web, but these books highlight the smaller changes inherent in our everyday life and which are so easy to overlook.

Above: Ilfracombe, 1964. Ilfracombe is the biggest resort on the North Devon coast and it developed as a result of the coming of the railways. This view of the town was taken from a hill known as the Tors and shows part of the centre of the town. There are several Victorian buildings to be seen. The building with the striped spire is the church of St Philip and St James.

Left: Ilfracombe, 2006. This photograph was taken in pouring rain which has reduced the distance clarity. However, while the church continues to dominate the centre of the scene, some changes are immediately obvious.

The building on the immediate right of the 1964 view – the Ilfracombe Hotel – has been demolished. On the hotel's site there is now a centre called the Landmark. This comprises externally two concrete towers (one of which is featured here), which are meant to represent sandcastles. Within the Landmark centre are housed the museum, tourist office and a theatre. The Landmark is now (2006) eight years old. Also demolished is the first building on the left of the 1964 photograph. This was the old theatre called the Victoria Pavilion, albeit it also had some 1960s additions.

Maria Pia

MANGIARE
ITALIANO

Mangiare Italiano

MARIA PIA

*translated by Richard Cross
and Richard Klein*

PHOTOGRAPHY SAL CRISCILLO

Penguin Group

Mangiare Italiano
CONTENTS

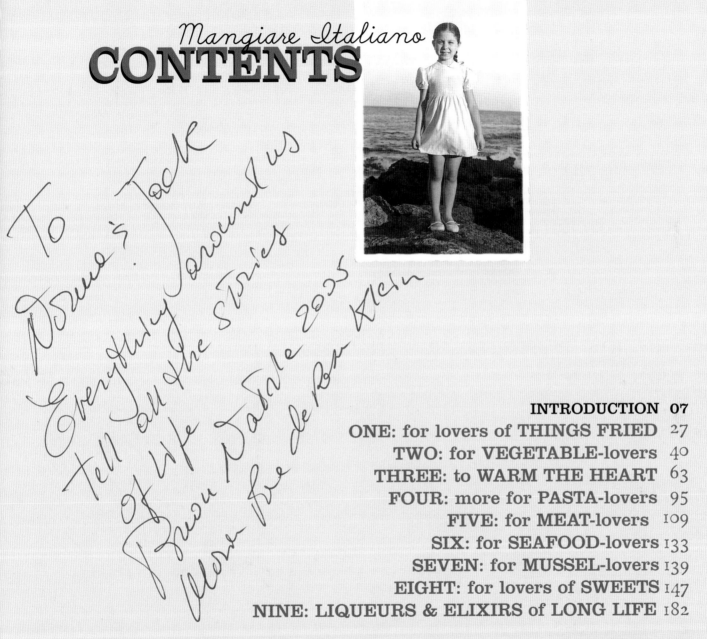

To
Donna & Jack
Everything around us
Tell all the stories
of life
Buon Natale 2005
More love de Rosa Klein

PRODUZ
ITALIA

Mangiare Italiano
INTRODUCTION

I remember once walking through the alleyways of Lecce, and being overcome by the feeling that it was pulsating with life and colour, even though the intense heat of the summer afternoon had emptied the streets. No one, but no one dared to venture outside. Benign games of shadows and shapes were being played out in front of my eyes, and I thought of those early master builders. They were the architects and sculptors; the brilliant artists of the Lecce-style baroque, so exuberant yet full of grace. They used hand-held chisels to work the local stone, called *carparo*, and turned it into gracious buildings, churches, balconies, statues (of saints, men, angels, even animals and fruit), columns, arches and porticoes.

Lecce has a magical atmosphere in the early evening and at night when everything is calm. Walking there with my daughters and husband, I saw that they too were transported back in time by the surroundings. I could sense that we were all stockpiling images of stratified history that was alive before our eyes. Like ghosts, the musicality of the dialects spoken by my people closed in around me as I listened and picked up the subtlety of their speech, like sweet music carried on the breeze.

Something always slipped through the hands of the constant line of aggressors who invaded and occupied Lecce over the centuries. Those who ruled over us have always written books on history and art. Thus in this tormented land of Salento, history and art have flourished together, the course of one leaving its mark on the other.

I love you and always will, my dear subjugated land. I know that I belong to you and I dedicate this book to you – your red, fertile earth. You have unerringly fed your people with your wheat and your oil, and like a mother you generously lavish your fruits on whoever asks.

LECCE

I see you, I remember you,
Memories being awakened are pouring salt
from my eyes.
I can feel you, I remember you,
My blood runs through your Earth.
I hear you, I remember you,
Your Sea is a blanket of clear silk.
I will meet you again, I know you,
You'll make me dance, you'll make me free.

DARA KLEIN

La mia citta Lecce e qualcosa su di me

MY CITY LECCE & SOME THINGS ABOUT ME

Lecce lies in the south of Italy, close to Greece -- in the heel of the boot, otherwise known as the Salento Peninsula, which is surrounded by the Adriatic Sea on one side and the Ionian Sea on the other. The first-time visitor to Lecce is bound to be struck by its architectural style. It is a baroque city like no other. Contributing to its uniqueness is the use of the local stone, also known as *pietra leccese*, which is a mix of limestone and sandstone. All of Lecce's buildings, palaces, churches and monuments are crafted from it, creating a triumph of baroque style and contrasts of lightness and darkness. Everything sparkles, especially on hot summer days when the entire city takes on a golden-white hue.

An expert analysis carried out in 1820 by Michele Milano concluded that there were traces of bone in the stone's composition, which led him to speculate that these were bones of marine animals. The stone is mined from the earth around Lecce and is used not only for construction, but also by artists and sculptors as their medium of expression.

It was once used to make huge cisterns, known as *le pile*, where olive oil was stored. My grandmother, Donna Luisa Santese Valentini, was the proud owner of several of the largest in the area. She called them *posture* (which comes from the Latin *positura* meaning 'to place'-- because they were so heavy, they were not meant to be moved). They fascinated me when I was small, when I accompanied her servants as they carried out their weekly task of replenishing the olive-oil supplies. The cisterns were situated to the left of the entrance to her grand home, in one of the many rooms leading down to its extensive cellars. Houses like that do not exist anymore.

Lecce was built from an area settled by the *Messapi*, the original, pre-Roman inhabitants of that part of Italy. It later became a Roman outpost and would likely have been a small village or suburb of the nearby city of Rudiae, where the Roman poet Quinto Ennio was born. Towards the end of the second century BC the city, now known as Lupiae, was a Roman military post. During the time of Emperor Hadrian

(AD 117–138), the great Roman amphitheatre was built and Lecce became one of the busiest centres in the Adriatic, remaining under Roman control for about five centuries.

Invasion upon invasion has created multiple layers of history in this city. The Greeks, Romans, Goths, Byzantines, Normans, Swabian League, Angevins and Aragonians each left their own cultural stamp. But it was the Arabs (in AD 838) who were responsible for the largest number of atrocities. Innocents were slaughtered and even today the language carries a memory of those times with the children's cry, 'Mum, the Turks are coming, run, we must save ourselves!' With the Byzantines also came monks who practised and introduced Greek rites. This had a notable influence on the church in Puglia until 1059, when the Normans brought a return to the rites of the Latin Church. With the Norman domination the peak of chivalric culture was reached, which takes us up to the Middle Ages. In the 14th century Lecce became prosperous through its commercial activities, and it was the centre of a cultural richness that has always characterised that part of Italy.

The arrival of Emperor Charles V (1500–52) saw the beginning of the Renaissance. The architecture of the period was influenced by the castle built in honour of the emperor, along with the Arch of Triumph and the belt of city walls. In this period Lecce confirmed itself as an artistic and cultural centre of notable importance. This was the moment when Lecce was enriched by many incredible buildings, turning it into a very refined and elegant city.

I recommend a visit to Lecce to anyone, whether as a tourist who already knows Italy, or as a first-time visitor. It is an area with a rich variety of dialects; there is also a group of 13 villages – the Grecia Salentina – where a type of archaic Greek is still spoken. It also keeps its traditions, values and habits, and these are clearly reflected in its gastronomy.

Morciano di Leuca, where I was born, is situated only a few kilometres from where the Adriatic and Ionian Seas meet. On my mother's side I have blood ties to the Aragon aristocracy. I have cousins who still live in the Castello di Morciano – an extraordinary building which still strongly evokes another age. My cousin Massimo welcomes anyone who loves culture, art, history and food to the castle. He offers accommodation as well as visits by appointment to anyone who wants to enjoy a truly special holiday. One day I would like to take my friends from New Zealand over there, to discover both the diversity and communality between the two cultures.

My mother, when she married in 1947, did not even know how to boil an egg. She was an only child of an aristocratic family. She was taught how to paint, play the piano and entertain guests. Domestic servants took care of all the chores. Italian society changed radically after Word War II, and as a result she had to roll up her sleeves. In other words, she had

to get by using her own abilities, and she had to accept that her children needed more than just an education at exclusive schools; they had to live a working life and take on responsibilities, just like everyone else.

I grew up in the shadow of that glorious past, which is also part of the history of wider Italy. Tomasso Pedio, a Leccese historian, once wrote about the importance of understanding one's own history, in order not to be subjected to the same problems in the future. My personal history is also the history of many of my friends, born, like me, in that part of Italy. We share the common bond of an illustrious history, derived from a stock of defunct noble families. And perhaps we each have an innate sense of survival in our hearts which distinguishes us; and a passion, true consciousness and respect for the times that once were.

Cooking has long been one of my many passions, along with politics, theatre, fashion and art. At times for me, cooking has meant starting at ten in the morning and finishing at five the next morning, seven days a week. It has been a mission, especially when juggled with mothering two small children. Fortunately, my husband Richard has always been understanding and helpful. I remember the time when I was cooking in a restaurant in the Apennines of Emilia-Romagna, close to the Garfagnana Valley in Tuscany. It was there that I discovered the beauty of cooking and talking –

chatting about anything and everything (as I believe only we women can), not only about food, but also about any problems of the day. It was also there that I discovered how there is no distinction between work and free time. I also developed a discipline in the search for both perfection and the desire to seek something different as an expression of who I am. It was also a place where the values of life were not measured solely in relation to the Almighty Dollar. There was a personal ethic; a respect for oneself and for what one does which does not bear comparison to any salary.

Cooking for me is a passion; it is creation, and it is something that takes me back in time, to my roots. To some, this has all but been lost, but not for me. It seems that everything to do with gastronomy is being touted as a first-time discovery, but for cultures like mine with an ancient history, food is an important thread that links us to the past, and I have connected it to my present, and my future. As I see it, my cooking skills and ideas will always come to me naturally, because they are my heritage.

Cooking and food have been the greatest influences on my life, helping me understand clearly who I am, and where I am going. After 53 years I have come to appreciate that money is only a bait, and just like shoal fish, there are those who get caught and those who don't!

CAFFE' DELL' ANFITEATRO

Grano
Pelato

Cibo, tradizioni, storie e cultura di terra mia e di Maria Pia

MARIA PIA'S LECCE – food, tradition, history & culture

I have always been fascinated by the way a society's culture can be understood through its gastronomy and traditions. I believe there is no better way to interpret and comprehend the secrets and nuances of life. And so, I would like to present *la mia cucina* – my kitchen, my cooking. It is in part a description of traditions, oral histories, places, people, events, while the rest is from . . . myself. Whether I call myself a chef (or *maestra di cucina*, master of the kitchen, to use a fairly new Italian term) or just simply *cuoca*, a cook, it doesn't really matter! The recipes I have gathered come from living sources – people who have been a part of my life and with whom my encounters, even when brief, have always been intensely fulfilling.

To my mind, it is misleading to speak of the *cucina Italiana*, Italian cuisine, categorised as it usually is into three regions – northern, central and southern. Every single region of Italy (of which there are 20), every single city, every single family, has its own distinctive way of interpreting the produce that comes from its land. There is, however, one thing in common for everyone in this process of interpretation, which is an identity forged from a sense of historical belonging. It has become the Italian tradition – the flavour of love and passion.

Therefore, my attempt to recognise the past in this manner represents not only a pleasure for the palate, but above all a means of conserving traditional knowledge. This heritage originates from the lives around me, as well as my own. Our past is also made up of century upon century of invasions from the races and nations surrounding Italy. However, this has had the advantage of setting in motion a kind of exchange, which in turn has resulted in a special diversity that is part of the true heritage of traditional Italian cuisine. You could even say it has been a blessing.

Because Italy is such a matriarchal society, the ties between women and cooking have not been confined to the family, but extend to places such as the *trattoria* and *osteria* (eateries and taverns). The names *trattoria* and *osteria* are synonymous with a place where the flavours and tastes of traditional dishes are served in correspondingly simple but always highly personable premises: straw-bottom chairs around worn old wooden tables and *piatti poveri*, the so-called 'poor dishes', which are made from simple, inexpensive ingredients. These dishes are, however, also rich in the love the cook has inherited from his or her origins. In this context, people talk openly and with compassion about their daily lives; so along with the food, cooked with simplicity and affection, all problems, big and small, are also put on the table. The dishes are certainly simple, but they are made with style and are abundant in healthy ingredients. These dishes owe their existence to the intelligence and resourcefulness of rustic people. From my contemporary vantage point, this is the ideal place to start discovering these recipes.

This book is therefore a journey into the history not only of Italy, but of every single cook; it focuses mainly on my region – Puglia – and in particular on the Salento Peninsula. In writing it, I have had the chance to re-evaluate a culture, my culture, which continues to surprise me, and which can hold its own against any of the latest trends in international cuisine. It is a culture, moreover, that seemed to know how to wait for its moment to be 'discovered' and, above all, understood. I hope to kindle a little curiosity in anyone who has a longing to rediscover a place in his or her memory, or for those eagerly setting out on a journey into the unknown – perhaps to the Mediterranean, where I come from. It is my wish, through this book, to also revisit my past, while at the same time translating it into something fresh and new.

I regard myself as an instinctive person, especially when I am in contact with an element very close to me – fire – and, more specifically, the stovetop! My real energy comes from cooking. It is almost an antidote to sadness and boredom. Joy and happiness, moments of love; aspects of me that I am able to express very well through the age-old art that woman has inherited from the Stone Age. Men went to hunt and women prepared, almost magically, their food.

It is remarkable how, from the most ancient cultures onwards, woman has remained anonymous while cooking to appease the hunger of uncountable families comprising her children and, sometimes, more than one husband. Now, in the name of all these anonymous women throughout history, I have carried out my own research which I would like to be able to pass on to others.

This book is the result of research not only into recipes, but also people – people who have recognised the value of, and kept a depository of, authentic and original gastronomic experiences. All this is presented against the backdrop of the enchanting landscape of my Italy or, at least, the Italy I once knew.

Writing this book has been hard work, but it has also been a pleasure. I have discovered how from one kilometre to the next, even the most traditional recipes can vary because every woman, every family, adapts them in their own way and, naturally, each one asserts that their own way of doing things is the right way.

'Food' corresponds to climate, culture, and the differing identities within that culture, which you sometimes can't create beyond the geographic limits of where it is consumed. This is because the base ingredients are so closely linked to what is produced locally, and some dishes are unable to be replicated exactly elsewhere. With recipes like these, I have noted variations that work well with easy-to-find ingredients.

This is a practical book of recipes, compiled with care, though I believe that the moment a recipe becomes 'fixed' in writing it becomes somewhat betrayed. The recipes come from a variety of regional Italian specialities. They evoke pleasurable feelings and memories of food I have tasted from every part of Italy, a country with so much diversity in its climate, geography, history and culture. I hope that I am able to contribute to safeguarding this precious inheritance from a civilisation noted for being convivial and expressive, which I see threatened by the use of the label 'Italian' to describe all manner of creatively improvised dishes which, in fact, are not Italian at all.

Land and sea, here, have known only true quiet and peace . . . or . . . war! In times of peace, the earth remains immobile under the summer heat, which blends with the sultry buzzing of cicadas, 30°C or more in the shade. This is the red-earthed Mediterranean 'bush'. Evergreen trees and shrubs endure extended exposure to the sun and the impact of the winds laden with African sand and the salty deposits of seawater. The highest rainfall occurs during the restless autumn and spring; interrupted by the summer season, which is normally dry and very sunny.

I used to love to venture along the country paths of my family's property. Spring was the best time to admire the chromatic explosion of iris, gladioli, sea onions and wild Mediterranean orchids. Not to mention all the other wild perennial herbs, too numerous to list, that played a central role in our cooking. And how could I forget the joy of smelling the perfumes released from the resins and oils of shrubs and bushes such as rockrose and myrtle – a tremendous and spontaneous blossoming of species, accompanied by a profusion of essences.

Most people in Italy consider this, my beautiful Salento Peninsula, to be impoverished of appreciable vegetation because of the apparent lack of lakes and important rivers – and possibly also because everyone considers Puglia to be *sitibona*, a place where people die of thirst. And to think that the entire region was so covered by forests that Frederick II of Hohenstaufen, Holy Roman Emperor from 1215–50 (and who also led the fifth crusade to the Holy Land and became King of Jerusalem), chose this area to train hunting falcons, and placed severe prohibitions on hunting and cutting wood, and instituted a mounted corps of forest guards!

This is a place where strips of rocks emerge along the coast, making it easy to misread the true expanse of the land where the vegetation runs wild and largely untamed. This is the *macchia* or Mediterranean bush overwhelmed by *gariga* – a hardy, indigenous plant made up of underground bulbs, which store water in order to survive. My father pointed these out to me when we went for walks for pleasure, or to inspect the work carried out by the workers on our land. One variety of the *gariga* plant is known as *spurchia*, which everyone used to eat greedily for its bittersweet taste and which, seasoned with olive oil, lemon and bread we children savoured until the last mouthful. What memories! *Spurchia*, I have discovered, has been decimated by chemical fertilisers that the farmers used instead of manure to the extent that it is now very difficult to find. Small signs such as these give me the feeling that the legacies of the past need our help, otherwise they will disappear in the name of 'progress', for want of a better name.

Such is the case of the *asfodelo*, or flowering lily, which thrives in extremely rocky and dry soil. And, still, the *gariga* awakes from winter lethargy when the gramineous plants push their way through and the tenderest threads of grass emerge, forming the softest meadows of velvet, followed by the sprouting of a stupendous variety of orchids. My earliest memories of adolescent love are beautifully entwined with such meadows.

My memory of the arrival of the balmy spring is also linked to daisies and saffron with its yellow crocus flowers, as well as what we called *Le scarpine della Madonna* – the Madonna's little shoes – as white and delicate as tissue paper. I also remember rows of artichokes, stretching out further than the eye could see. I will never forget my tongue turning completely black because I had eaten an improbable amount of raw, small artichokes, straight after being picked. That bittersweet taste of the artichoke, so sweet and yellow, which when put in the mouth and mixed with saliva forged an orgy of unique tastes. Such profound and distinct tastes I have never again experienced in my life from any other food or

ingredient, no matter how exotic its origin.

It is from that particular taste of artichokes in springtime that I recognise my roots to my Salento, to my Lecce, to my sea of Leuca.

In Leuca, stories and legends are intertwined so tightly that it is difficult to know where their respective threads begin. Leuca can mean 'white', or 'light', or simply 'cape' or 'promontory'. In ancient times, according to the geographies of Homer and the navigators who recognised and mapped some of the more evident visible features on the coast, it had names such as White Cape (probably for its intense light from morning to evening, which to this day continues to be intense), Black Rocks and so on. Leuca was the first port of call for ships arriving from Greece, and it then became the Iapigio promontory, from the name of the first inhabitants. The founder, according to one of the legends, was Idomeneo, returning from the destruction of Troy. It was also where Aeneas landed, as the poet Virgil affirms with the citation in the third book of the *Aeneid*.

In keeping with another ancient legend, Saint Peter too landed on these rocks, on his way from the East to preach Christianity, with many others then following in his wake.

In fact, hidden amongst the pines, on the large piazza of the *Santurario della Madonna* (Sanctuary of Our Holy Lady) you will find an iron cross with two overlapping keys. This is the *croce petrina*, or Cross of Remembrance, placed there during the Mariano Congress of 1949. Tradition has it that on that spot Saint Peter began his preachings. Legend also has it that the Apostle was so struck by the beauty of the place that he decreed that everyone had to go to Leuca at least once in their lives, almost as if it was like an antechamber before arriving in Heaven.

The *Sancturario Sancta Maria de finibus terrae* rises on the rock which is the exact point where two seas join: the Adriatic and the Ionian. According to the historian Giacomo Arditi, Leuca was first settled by the Phoenicians, an ancient people inhabiting the narrow coastline that extends from Lebanon to the Mediterranean. At the site of the *Santurario della Madonna*, a pagan temple dedicated to the goddess Minerva once stood. An altar from that original temple still remains today. The Sanctuary is the most celebrated spiritual centre in Puglia, and the people's devotion to it continues to be enormous.

La festa in onore della Madonna di Leuca, protettrice dei mari

THE CELEBRATION IN HONOUR OF THE MADONNA OF LEUCA, PROTECTOR OF THE SEAS

The fishermen of Leuca are the protagonists of this feast. They carry the hefty statue of the *Madonna di Leuca* to the sea and place her on a fishing boat which is then followed by a multitude of smaller boats, decorated with flowers, coloured ribbons and climbing shrubs, all to the accompaniment of the ever-present local bands. Music and odes are performed and supplications are invoked from participants and those who follow the procession to the sea. Everything takes place at sea which, as far as I can recall, has always been as flat as a table every year on that day, as if the procession has the protection of peace and tranquillity at this place where the Adriatic and Ionian seas converge. The Madonna of Leuca is seen as the mother and protector of all who entreat her. The procession lasts several hours and finishes up around sunset. Naturally, as evening falls, so begin the celebrations held in each family home.

Under a sky littered with stars and the sea still invitingly warm for a last swim, I can't recall how many times I have celebrated the banquet of 15 August at the house of my grandmother, Donna Luisa Santese Valentini. A noblewoman, she learnt the art of supreme hospitality from the youngest age. Under her guidance and through her connections, servants and expert cooks carried out this gastronomic rite with its own precise order of serving.

The southern tradition is closer to what is known as French Service – the old cuisine style, from the days of the Court. This entails bringing a large number of dishes to the table at the same time in a grandiose display of abundance and luxury.

In one single serving everything that could be offered is brought to the table. Dominating the centre of the table is a large bowl painted in traditional Salento-style designs, from which everyone then serves themselves using their own cutlery. The bowl is full of fresh pasta made from hard durum wheat. Following this course comes an unbelievable quantity and variety of fruit (both fresh and dried), along with stalks of celery and fennel bulbs. These palate-cleansing vegetables complete the meal and help to send down much more willingly that last glass of wine.

What are now called *antipasti*, or appetisers, were originally called simply *cumpanaggi*, in the sense that they were ideal for accompanying bread – the famous *pane pugliese*, the king of all the breads made from hard wheat!

A great variety of olives are also placed on the table, all different in colour, quality and style of preparation. Local varieties with untranslatable names like *celline*, *casciole* and *saracine* are commonly preserved in brine. They are picked from the olive tree when perfectly blackened, hence their name in dialect – *ulie niure*, or black olives. In fact, an old saying goes: 'On the Immacolata, the *celline* matures.' The Immacolata, or the Day of the Virgin, is the celebration of 8 December, which is when the *celline* matures and can be picked from the tree.

Other types of olives have to be sweetened in a mixture of lime and ashes, until they became tender, before being put in brine with bay leaves and wild fennel (*Foeniculum piperitum e vulgare*), which sprouts up everywhere. Then there is the large trunk-ended variety from Taranto, called *cazzarola*, or the *cerasole* from Tricase, or the sweet olives from Barbarano. The most common variety is called *pasùla* or *fasùla* and is large and round. But the best were the *San Agostino*, better known by the name *d'Andria*; the *pesciolen*, and the *leccino* (or *sperone di gallo* – chicken's crest).

For centuries all of these local varieties of olives have adorned the feast table on this special day. They are traditionally presented in characteristic dishes along with fried, fresh chilli peppers, oregano, garlic, sprigs of *Pistacia lentiscus* (also known as mastic gum), green lemon zest, salt and extra-virgin olive oil. Sometimes salted capers, which have been soaked in water, are also added.

The feast comprises 15 servings in honour of 15 August. All the fresh seafood and fish that the fishermen have caught from their boats during the day is prepared and presented:

1. Calamari salad with mint
2. Sea urchins with pucce – small sourdoughbread with black olives
3. Stewed octopus in typical terracotta dishes called tutto paro
4. Oven-baked cuttlefish with potatoes
5. Scapece di pupiddhi – small, whole fish which are breaded, fried and preserved with saffron and vinegar
6. Black mussels, breaded and baked
7. Black-mussel salad with cucumber melon
8. Leuca-style eggplant served on a large baking dish
9. La tieddha – a Pugliese specialty made with mussels, potatoes and rice
10. Stuffed zucchini flowers
11. Stewed eggplant
12. Sagne Cannullate – an enormous dish of handmade pasta served with fresh tomato sauce, basil and fermented ricotta cheese known as ricotta scanta
13. Fish soup (in a thin broth)
14. Aquaesale – salad with crumbs of dry bread, tomato, red chillies, new potatoes, salt and extra-virgin olive oil

And to finish, the 15th course comprises an unbelievable quantity of fruit: from watermelon to melons; intensely fragrant white and yellow peaches (*percochi*), sliced and macerated in glasses of cold *Rosato del Salento* (local rosè wine) figs of every colour, shape and variety; and *Fichi d'India*, or prickly pears. Finally, to conclude the meal and cleanse the palate, more stalks of celery (or *laccio*, in dialect) are served.

Towards midnight the fireworks begins, their reflections visible in the Bay of Leuca, the sea as smooth as a millpond, tranquil but balmy – so tempting to indulge in a last swim before going to sleep. And swim we would, but not until the moment when the sun peeked out to announce the arrival of yet another summer's day of 30°C or more.

MARIA PIA

Ricordi ... ricordi
MEMORIES . . . MEMORIES

It is summer and 35°C in the shade. It is so hot, muggy and the cicadas never cease their singing! I am on a tiny train of the Italian State Railways, in the south-east. The train consists of only one carriage, and I'm in it by myself. These days hardly anyone uses this means of transport anymore, which is both slow and romantic. I am about 20 minutes away from Otranto and the sea. Leaving from Maglie, in the hinterland, the small town where my 83-year-old mother lives; a beautiful and tenacious woman, an artistic, intrepid businesswoman, a noblewoman of the south, and at the same time mother of a good seven children. I think that it is nostalgia that has brought me to take this part of the journey by train, rather than by car. It is a unique and pleasant way to rediscover my memories.

It's so hot that my amber-coloured skin is breathing the nectar of that dry heat; I feel revitalised and full of energy. My clothes of rough natural-coloured linen, made as in the olden days from woven cloth, highlight my tanned skin and the chestnut colour in my hair, which has also become warm and curly too thanks to the hot, dry air. Life pulsates inside me. I feel happy and immensely beautiful.

Like a cuttlefish, my own colours have changed naturally, camouflaging me with the hues of nature that surround me. I open all the windows of the train, putting my face up to one of them to let my eyes do the travelling! I feel them filling with tears, tears from the shadows of my memories. For further than my eyes can see, rows and rows of olive trees pass by, ancient, probably 500, 600 or 700 years old. What stories they could tell!

The train pulls with it peoples' joys, hopes and bad moods, as it has through the days and years over this distance. Its rhythm consoles me. It's like being in a cradle, and one's powers of logic are mingled with the sleep of memories . . . and . . . I don't have the slightest idea anymore where the train is going! All of a sudden white bell towers of churches appear, fluorescent-like in the bright sunlight, that Mediterranean sunlight that reflects in the white of the local stone. A gust of warm wind hits me and passes through the train's open window. It startles me so much that my heart skips a beat. The smell of smoke, a particular burning smell from the stubbles of smoking wheat, lacerates my nostrils. Oh, how well I recall this smell. A return, a return through memory empties me and leaves me breathless.

Summer after summer, I worked alongside the people who tilled the land. My parents owned a lot of land on which wheat was grown. To further our education, mother and father made us work during the *mietitura*, or harvest, because only through knowing the meaning of hard work, could we shape a real knowledge of ourselves. While my friends were at the beach swimming, sunbathing and flirting, my brothers and sisters and I learnt the hard discipline of working in the fields alongside the farm workers. At this point in time I feel I owe my parents a debt of gratitude for instilling in me not only a sense of discipline, but also a way of learning about the produce of the land.

In September 1961, my closest brother Pierluigi died at the age of 13 – of sunstroke, we thought at the time. We had been working all day under the hot, late-summer sun harvesting grapes. The wine of that year is still remembered as one of the best because of that long hot summer. On returning home Pierluigi had a very high fever. In fact, he had contracted meningitis and died a few hours later.

I understood then how great a gift life is. I had a feeling that I was no longer a child. I was only ten at the time. From that day on I have always been scared to stay under the sun without protection. The sun is an important element of nature, but its immense power means we must have much more respect for it.

My brothers and sisters and I used to stay with the workers, who were paid for the whole harvest season, until sunset every day. There were 50 to 100 people who were all fed breakfast and lunch, which consisted of *diavolicchi*, fried spicy red chilli peppers, and *frise*, a twice-baked bread softened with water and accompanied with plenty of tomatoes and extra virgin olive oil. I remember all the names of the varieties of wheat – *cappello*, *appulo*, *creso*, *patrizio*, *grifone*, *capeiti*, *valforte*, *valgeraldo* and so on. Most were local varieties, some of which are perhaps no longer grown, as the seeds have disappeared.

Through my father Gregorio I received the highest respect for the land. His family, who also had connections with the church, had for generations owned substantial amounts of land. Having studied in his early years with the Jesuits, a religious order that 'looked after' the education of the offspring of the most important families in the area, he gained an understanding of the importance of land and its ties with the agriculture of the southern regions. He also understood the importance of the cultural identity of Puglia and the development of this region for the cultivation of vines, olives and vegetables.

For hundreds of years Puglia was exploited by the merchants and businessmen coming from different areas in Italy – such as the Veneto, Piedmont, Tuscany, Campania and Lazio – because it was a 'hotbed' of high-quality products which they acquired at next-to-nothing prices. So the profits did not remain in Puglia, where hard labour had produced them, but went into the pockets of these middlemen of questionable integrity.

Fortunately things have changed since then. The products are now processed locally and sold with the tag 'made in Puglia'. My poor father didn't live long enough to see the revaluation of our land! I thank him, however, for having given me a respect for the truth, and how it is expressed. During his university studies in Bologna, he cultivated a taste for the fine cuisine of that region, so famous throughout the world. He would never have imagined, at the time we children were helping work the land, that one of his three daughters would end up being involved for a good 12 years in the passion of cooking right there in the *grassa Emilia-Romagna* (*Emilia-Romagna* – 'the fat one').

I cooked with some wonderful people who upheld the highest professional standards, and from whom I learned the secrets of the art of *sfoglia*, or rolling pasta dough to obtain the right consistency. It is important to use a proper *mattarello* or rolling pin – not one of those small contraptions with red handles, which look like dolls' toys! Nowadays hardly any young Italian chefs learn this skill. They all use pasta machines and, as a result, the fresh pasta is not the same.

The name Emilia-Romagna evokes places like Bologna, Modena and Parma, all of which are rich in culinary sophistication and the cradle of such famous products as Balsamic vinegar, Parma *prosciutto*, Parmesan cheese, *tortellini*, *lasagna* and so on.

For over 12 years I had the good fortune to learn the secrets and live with *gli Emiliani*, the Emilians, people of incredible generosity and industriousness, to the extent that I felt right at home with them. I prepared an incredible quantity of *tortellini*, all hand-made – from rolling the dough to making the fillings – with 20 to 30 women from Emilia, the *rezdòre*, as they were called. Their ability to shape a miniscule square of *tortellini* on their little finger, or use the rolling pin to make the dough as thin as possible, was evidence of years and years of experience and professionalism, which took me back in time, from generation to generation.

From my mother Gilda Valentini I inherited a profound knowledge of flour. In fact, she was one of the first to recognise the culinary importance of the fresh pasta from Puglia. She had a pasta shop called Derval, a name derived from combining the first three initials of my parents' surnames: DERazza and VALentini. I learned from her how to use flour in the best way, which was the method we adopted.

The flour used at the Derval factory was made from wheat grown on our family land. Grain after grain, the buckets were filled with white durum wheat, which was then taken to the mill in the small town of Patù, close to Leuca. Our pasta was made not only for retail sales, but also for supplying some of the best restaurants in the area, as well as for special occasions, such as weddings, baptisms and funerals. The pasta was always prepared specially for the occasion.

The starting point for any type of pasta from Salento is always the same: fresh semola, that is, ground durum wheat (sometimes mixed with pearl-barley flour), warm water and a pinch of salt. NO EGGS! You simply sieve the flour well and make a mound on the kneading table (preferably made of marble or other stone, otherwise of wood), pour the water into a crater formed in the middle and make a ball of dough, which is then kneaded. The amount of water will vary according to the type of flour used, as different types of wheat have different protein contents, which will affect the rate of absorption. Always leave the mixture to rest, ensuring that it remains soft.

In the olden days pasta was made in small thread-like shapes. A type called *lagane* was eaten with a sweet sauce, made from honey and cinnamon, and cooked in milk. When any of us children were sick, my mother would immediately prepare these treats that induced us to sleep. I still prepare a few of these types of pasta in my *trattoria* in Wellington. It is an act of creativity and joy which transports me back to the tastes and smells of my Puglia.

When I was a child, not a day would pass without a plate of fresh pasta on the family table. Naturally, the pasta was always of the highest quality as it was made from freshly ground flour and served with produce from our own land. There were six kids, all full of energy. Problems with acne, asthma, obesity and skin problems simply didn't exist for us. Unfortunately today's adolescents do indeed face these problems, in part from consuming all manner of processed ingredients, which are slowly poisoning them.

Nowadays food isn't food; it is only a means of making money, often to the detriment of public health. We don't need more hospitals and medicine, but more education on eating habits – in the family, in schools, in supermarkets. We need to have the courage to abolish certain products that are not fit to eat or drink, and to have more people who know about these things. It would make everyday life easier for every one of us.

We shouldn't let ourselves be carried away by the allure and flattery of commercialisation, whereby the more a product is advertised the more it seems to be accepted. For centuries, food for the body, soul and spirit was created on the stovetop, through the knowledge of people who loved us. Food like this was never 'heat and serve' or ready to eat in a minute.

We should revel in the joy of cooking, even of simple dishes, and cook with real ingredients which come from the land and sea. If we do this, we'll all live to be a hundred! I think that where there is an abundance of good food from the land and where the skies are clear, people are consequently happy and more open with one another.

My wish for tomorrow is to bring back what we don't have today – peace and a life in which the values of those who live close to the land are recognised and appreciated. It's not petrol we eat, but rather bread. It is up to each person to make up his or her own mind about this.

People from Puglia have in common with the Greeks, our close neighbours, colours, flavours and tastes for things that are true and pure, things that come spontaneously under the sun as they appear in front of us. We react the same way to nature and whatever surrounds us; you can tell straight away from our faces what we are thinking. We are frank, we say what we think, and we do not stab people in the back.

My father Gregorio, who was a lawyer and also a very sensitive human being, often said to me: 'You, Pia, have all the qualities to make a good lawyer, except you do one thing a good lawyer must never do – you think aloud! In fact, you scream and shout your opinions like a priestess of Bacchus!'

As I write these words it is raining outside, a northerly wind shatters the streets of Wellington, lifting leaves, bark and hair. It seems as if at any moment the city could be ripped from the earth and flung away. From my window I see the Old Saint Paul's Church all white and with trees immaculately surrounding it. They too are being beaten by the wind from every direction. But then I feel a sudden calm, for a few seconds, which leaves the air immobile. I feel like praying for my Uncle Agostino, my father's brother, who died last year. He is survived by his wife Bianca, an incredible narrator of history and events of times gone by.

Zio Agostino was a very good-looking man with great natural strength, both physical and mental. For this reason some thought he was difficult, but in reality he was very simple in the sense that he saw everyone and everything in the same light. He was very sweet, and sometimes he even seemed to be a little naïve to me. Growing up and speaking to him, I understood that his gentle and simple nature were in fact the result of his optimistic character, rich with human warmth, but at the same time immensely strong.

Unfortunately, my uncle's generation was affected by World War II, when he was in the flower of youth. He experienced concentration camps in Germany and was held as a prisoner of war by the British in North Africa. But he survived, and victoriously so, because those experiences did not injure his soul or his spirit. Talking about some of those people and places, he said to me once: 'War is useless; it serves no purpose for anybody, nobody wins or loses, instead . . . anyone who survives rediscovers the true meaning of life, and the reason we are born! It makes you think again and you discover that you are a good person!'

One day on the battlefield, while he was on the front near the enemy line, he noticed a plant that he thought he recognised from home, growing right there in the rocks and bramble. He could not believe it was growing there, far away from his native Puglia! It was the alexanders or horse parsley (*Smyrnium olusatrum*), known in Leccese dialect as *zivirnia* or *zavirna*. This plant is found on untamed land where there is humidity; it grows in shady places. Its white, tender flowers are gathered, especially at Christmas when they are covered in batter and fried. I remember that the tender roots were also cooked on a grill over ashes or in the oven and then wrapped in tinfoil, – to be seasoned with olive oil or salt. The sharp, aromatic taste was enjoyed for centuries, until medieval times when celery appeared.

At the very moment when Uncle Agostino bent over to make sure it really was the wild plant he thought it was, a machine gun raked the area where he was, killing everybody except him. He survived because he had stopped to look more closely at the plant he had recognised. From that moment on he decided to name it holy *zivirnia*!

So here is a classic Puglian recipe for you to try – every family has its own variation – that was a particular favourite of Uncle Agostino.

I Panzerotti
DEEP-FRIED SAVOURY PASTRIES

These are from a series of fried yeasted pastries, a type of food that Mediterranean cuisine does so well. The dough mixture is interesting because it appears to be similar to a pizza dough, though it is not the same. Whatever filling you decide to use, I recommend adding one clove of garlic, finely chopped or crushed through a garlic press. *Panzerotti* can be served either hot or cold, and they make a great snack.

The Puglia *panzerotti* have different types of fillings:
1. Mozzarella, eggs, grated pecorino (sheep) cheese and chopped parsley
2. Ricotta, eggs and chopped parsley
3. Fried onion with a small amount of fresh tomato and a cheese called caciocavallo (a type of stretched cheese). Alternatively, you could use sweet or spicy provolone cheese
4. Fried onions, anchovies in oil, tomato, capers and parsley
5. Tuna in oil, cooked onion, parsley, tomato and capers

MAKES 10–12 PASTRIES

for the filling
300g BOCCONCINI MOZZARELLA (approximately 12 pieces), cubed
400g small TOMATOES (ideally CHERRY TOMATOES), diced
3 tablespoons EXTRA VIRGIN OLIVE OIL
1 tablespoon FRESH or DRIED OREGANO
1 clove GARLIC, chopped or crushed in a garlic press
2 teaspoons SEA SALT
freshly ground BLACK PEPPER to taste

for the dough
20g FRESH YEAST
200ml lukewarm WATER (see Maria Pia's tip, below)
400g DURUM-WHEAT FLOUR
a pinch of SALT

1 litre PURE OLIVE OIL for frying

to make the filling:
Season the mozzarella and diced tomatoes with the olive oil, oregano, garlic, salt and pepper and set aside.

to make the dough:
1. Dissolve the yeast in 3 tablespoons of the lukewarm water. On a suitable surface for kneading form a mound with the flour, sprinkle with a pinch of salt, and make a crater in the middle. Pour the yeast mixture into the centre, add the remaining water and begin to work the dough, forming a ball. Knead for 10 minutes.

2. Transfer to a bowl, cut a cross on top and cover with a clean, damp tea towel. Leave to rise for 1 hour in a warm place.

3. Using a rolling pin, roll out to a thickness of 2mm. Using an 8–10cm-diameter water or wine glass, cut out disks.

4. Cover half of each disk with the filling. Fold over the other half of the disk, forming a half-moon shape. Ensure that the pastry is tightly sealed and leave to set while heating the oil.

to make the pastries:
Heat the oil in a deep-frying pan over a moderate heat for approximately 15 minutes. Fry the half moons in the hot oil until golden brown, turning them over once. Drain on absorbent paper and serve.

Maria Pia's tips: The water required for the dough mixture varies, according to the type of flour used and the ambient temperature. You need to work out for yourself the right quantity. Don't be discouraged by failure. That is how you really learn to be a good cook!

To check whether the oil is hot enough for deep-frying, test a small piece of dough first. When the dough bubbles and rises to the surface, the oil is ready for deep-frying.

for lovers of things fried
CHAPTER ONE

Olive oil is a monounsaturated fat and contains many minerals as well as vitamins A and E. I have a huge passion for extra virgin olive oil. I like to try different types of extra virgin olive oil with salads. Personally, I prefer olive oil that is a deep, dark yellow (and which also has a strong flavour) as opposed to green-coloured olive oil.

Many people treat wine in the same way I experiment with olive oil. Because every Italian dish has its own area of origin, the type of olive oil used must be consistent with the recipe.

There are many prejudices against frying. I do not like it too much either, but a well-fried dish is worth enjoying every now and then.

In Khandallah, I once had a takeaway shop and delicatessen from where I also did some catering as well. A fire broke out there once, which luckily did not cause too much damage. It started in a deep-fryer. Perhaps it did not like the olive oil being used, or maybe it was the olive oil that did not like being fried? Anyway, after that I decided to deep-fry in a normal pan, like my mother used to.

For deep-fried vegetables and pastries (sweet or savoury) – I prefer the less-expensive kind (also known as 'pure olive oil') which is particularly compatible with these ingredients.

Olive oil may seem a little bit more expensive than other vegetable oils, but since it cannot be genetically engineered it remains a much healthier choice.

To appreciate the real taste of extra virgin olive oil it is better to use it only raw as a condiment (for drizzling over foods or in salads).

When you have finished eating a fried dish, the taste of olive oil is immediately noticeable. I have had customers who have said that they recognise this whenever I have prepared a fried dish, as it is distinguished by a sweet, rounded flavour.

It is difficult for me to observe not only how many bad-quality fried dishes are eaten by teenagers nowadays, but that they are eaten almost every day. I see fried chips going into the mouths of teenagers all the time. Because they are starving, the moment they come out of school, these young people head for the nearest fish-and-chip shop, coming out with bulging packets.

This is an example of the consumption of badly-fried food. On the other hand, chips made at home can be something quite different. Parents, try making your own chips at home using good oil and encourage your children not to buy them too often!

Frittelle di San Martino
SAINT MARTIN'S FRITTERS

These fritters are traditionally served during the Christmas period, but I recall that at home they were often made for Saint Martin's day on 1 November, when they would be accompanied by hot-roasted chestnuts. Either way, we kids were crazy about them! These fritters were our favourite after-school snack, and even though they were fried, we never had problems with acne or being overweight. In fact, we were all skinny and full of energy.

MAKES ABOUT 20 FRITTERS

20g FRESH YEAST
220ml lukewarm WATER
400g WHEAT FLOUR, plus 50g for kneading
a pinch of SALT
2 tablespoons OLIVE OIL
20 ANCHOVY FILLETS preserved in oil, drained
FENNEL SEEDS
1 litre PURE OLIVE OIL for frying
WHITE PEPPER (optional)

1. Dissolve the yeast in 3 tablespoons of lukewarm water. On a suitable surface for kneading, form a mound with 400g flour, sprinkle with a pinch of salt, and make a crater in the middle. Pour the yeast mixture in the centre and add the remaining water, 1 tablespoon of olive oil and begin to work the dough, forming a ball. Knead for 10 minutes.

2. Transfer to a bowl, cut a cross shape on the top and cover with a clean, damp tea towel. Leave to rise for 1 hour in a warm place.

3. Knead for a further 10 minutes using the remaining flour and 1 tablespoon of oil.

4. Form dough into bread rolls 6cm long by 3cm thick. Make a 1cm slice along the length of each roll. Stuff with an anchovy fillet and a few fennel seeds, and pinch to close. Leave the rolls to rise in a warm place for a further 30 minutes.

5. Heat the oil in a deep-frying pan over a moderate heat for approximately 15 minutes. Fry the fritters on both sides. When they are golden brown, drain on absorbent paper. Sprinkle immediately with a little white pepper, if desired. Serve warm or cold.

Maria Pia's tip: To check whether the oil is hot enough for deep-frying, test a small piece of dough first. When the dough bubbles and rises to the surface, the oil is ready for deep-frying.

MARIA PIA

Panelle di farina di ceci fritte
FRIED CHICKPEA FLOUR STICKS

I remember my mother preparing this for us as an afternoon snack, which we ate between slices of bread with a few drops of lemon juice squeezed over them. Her mother-in-law (that is, my father's and Uncle Agostino's mother) had given her the recipe to make for her children, nephews and nieces. The tradition continues! Sometimes I also serve these as an antipasto with some grated pecorino cheese, olives and marinated mushrooms.

SERVES 6–8 (ANY EXCESS CAN BE EATEN THE DAY AFTER!)

400g CHICKPEA FLOUR

400ml WATER

2 tablespoons FENNEL SEEDS or ANISEEDS

2 tablespoons salt

2 tablespoons EXTRA VIRGIN OLIVE OIL, plus
5 additional tablespoons for greasing the work surface

1 litre PURE OLIVE OIL for frying

1. Place the chickpea flour into a saucepan. Add water, whisking continuously until a thick batter forms. Add the fennel seeds or aniseeds, salt and 2 tablespoons of olive oil. Place pan on the stove and cook over a medium heat for approximately 15 minutes, whisking constantly in the same direction.

2. Pour batter on to a marble slate (or alternative smooth work surface) greased with the additional extra-virgin olive oil. Smooth with a spatula to make a 5mm-thick layer. Leave to cool.

3. Cut into 5cm x 1cm sticks then deep-fry in hot oil. When the sticks are golden brown, drain on absorbent paper. These fried sticks can be served as part of a mixed antipasto plate with prosciutto, pickled vegetables and cheese.

Il gnocco fritto di Modena
GNOCCO FROM MODENA

For an Italian the use of the article *il* in front of *gnocco* usually seems strange as it is grammatically incorrect – it should be *lo*. But the use of *il* signals a dialect and the recipe is immediately recognisable as a classic from Modena.

In the shadows of the Ghirlandina (the tower which is the symbol of Modena), I lived with my husband Richard in an attic under the red roofs of an old house in the historic centre of town. When it snowed in winter, from the windows of our bedroom it seemed as if we were in the middle of the 14th century. From the age of three months, my daughter Astrid slept in a cot next to our bed which took up most of the bedsit. The magic of those moments is still inside me, especially when the swallows skipped over the roof tiles in spring, as if they wanted to pass from one window to the next.

Every day my little Astrid and I went to the covered market, which was in the *centro storico* (old town). It is a building with a small fountain in the middle, architecturally structured to bring absolute joy to all five senses. Stalls rich with every gift from God, tended with attention to the last detail, were lovingly arranged to entice the buyer. But it was also a place where everything happened – a theatre of life where stories, characters, cultures and food intertwined to create the script that is everyday life, right there in Modena. Everyone knew each other, it was impossible not to stop and have a chat, and at the same time you were invaded with the divine smells of bread, salami, peaches . . . and *gnocco fritto*. Because at that time we had very little money, I couldn't afford to spend it on a *gnocco*. But as I salivated over the thought of how much I would enjoy it, sometimes the urge was too strong. So Astrid and I would sometimes share that diamond-shaped fritter, stuffed with an incredible slice of Parma prosciutto, whose oiliness had almost melted because of the heat of the *gnocco*, producing a unique and unrepeatable union of gastronomy and aroma.

The *gnocco* can be enjoyed as a snack in the morning or in the late afternoon. They can also be eaten like a sandwich, with a filling of Parma prosciutto. The Modenese even eat them first thing in the morning along with a cappuccino!

SERVES 6

MARIA PIA

600g WHITE FLOUR
1 teaspoon SEA SALT
5 tablespoons EXTRA VIRGIN OLIVE OIL
30g PORK LARD, finely chopped until almost a paste
250ml SPARKLING WATER (at room temperature)
2 tablespoons lukewarm MILK
40g FRESH YEAST
1.5 litres PURE OLIVE OIL for frying

1. Place the flour on a baking board. Add the salt, extra virgin olive oil and the finely chopped lard.

2. In a bowl mix the sparkling water and milk together. Dissolve the yeast in the liquid. Add the liquid to the flour mixture and work the ingredients well. Shape pastry into a large ball, transfer to a bowl and cover with a clean, damp tea towel. Leave to rise for at least 1 hour in a warm place.

3. With a rolling pin, roll the pastry to a thickness of 3mm. Cut pastry into diamond shapes, approximately 12cm x 10cm, or slightly larger.

4. Heat the pure olive oil in a deep-frying pan over a moderate heat for approximately 15 minutes. Deep-fry *gnocci* for no more than 5 seconds on each side. Drain on absorbent paper. Serve hot.

Frittelle di verdura mista
MIXED VEGETABLE FRITTERS

A wide variety of vegetables can be used for this recipe, except capsicum which should never be batter-fried. This version of the recipe celebrates some favourite summer vegetables, in particular zucchini flowers.

SERVES 8

150g ZUCCHINI

150g SCALOPPINI or YELLOW ZUCCHINI

300g EGGPLANT (long and firm is best)

8 ZUCCHINI FLOWERS

1 litre PURE OLIVE OIL for frying

500g MESCLUN SALAD MIX

for the batter
2 free-range, organic EGG YOLKS

1 free-range, organic EGG WHITE

300g WHITE FLOUR

160g MILK

1 tablespoon freshly grated PARMESAN CHEESE

1 clove GARLIC, chopped, or crushed in a garlic press

1 tablespoon MINT, finely chopped

1 tablespoon SALT and freshly ground BLACK PEPPER to taste

for the dressing
3 tablespoons WHITE WINE

3 tablespoons VINCOTTO

3 tablespoons LEMON JUICE

1. Dice the zucchini, scaloppini and eggplant into 2cm cubes. Remove the main pistil from the zucchini flowers. Prepare the batter (see below).

2. Heat the frying pan with the oil over a moderate heat for 15 minutes.

3. Begin frying the vegetables in batches, dipping them in the batter just before frying. Start with the zucchini flowers, then the zucchini, followed by the scaloppini and lastly the eggplant. Drain on absorbent paper.

4. Divide the mesclun among the individual plates and arrange the vegetables on top. Drizzle dressing over the vegetables.

to make the batter:
1. Separate the egg yolks and white. Leave the white to one side, as it will be beaten.

2. Whisk together all the batter ingredients, except the egg white, taking care not to let any lumps form.

3. In a separate bowl, beat the egg white until stiff and carefully fold into the batter.

to make the dressing:
1. Whisk the white wine, Vincotto and lemon juice together.

Maria Pia's tip: To obtain evenly shaped fritters, use a soup spoon to transfer the vegetables to the oil. Also, never salt the vegetables before frying, otherwise they become too watery.

Crocchette di fagioli borlotti con salsa di pomodorini

BORLOTTI-BEAN CROQUETTES WITH CHERRY-TOMATO SAUCE

I made this dish in my delicatessen in Khandallah, and it was also popular when I catered for various embassies in Wellington. This recipe, like the others in my book, has been shaped by the experience of hundreds of women who, from one kitchen to another, have enabled the ancient and traditional flavours of Italy to travel the world. These are not women with long, painted fingernails, but with hands marked with oil burns, almost like badges. It is not the recipe itself that makes great food, but how much of yourself you put into the recipe and its preparation. I learned how to make the cherry-tomato sauce in Imperia, Liguria, where it is also used to accompany their famous fried fish.

SERVES 8–10

MARIA PIA

for the croquettes
800g POTATOES, unpeeled

50g SPINACH

5 tablespoons EXTRA VIRGIN OLIVE OIL

250g tinned BORLOTTI BEANS, drained

1 clove GARLIC, finely chopped
or crushed in a garlic press

2 tablespoons SALT

3 free-range, organic EGG YOLKS

2 free-range, organic EGG WHITES

4 tablespoons PARMESAN CHEESE,
freshly grated

freshly ground BLACK PEPPER

a pinch of NUTMEG

1 cup FLOUR

3 cups BREADCRUMBS

1 litre PURE OLIVE OIL for frying

for the sauce
2 cloves GARLIC, finely chopped or
crushed

15 BASIL LEAVES, finely chopped

2 tablespoons ITALIAN PARSLEY, finely
chopped

1 small RED CHILLI PEPPER, left whole
(optional)

1 cup EXTRA VIRGIN OLIVE OIL

500g ripe CHERRY TOMATOES, halved

SALT to taste

to make the croquettes:

1. Boil the unpeeled potatoes.

2. In a separate pot, boil the spinach in a little water, then drain and chop coarsely.

3. Heat the extra virgin olive oil in a pan and add the cooked spinach, drained beans, garlic and 1 tablespoon of salt. Cook for 10 minutes over a moderate heat. Allow to cool, then blend in a food processor for 10 seconds.

4. Separate the eggs and set the whites aside in a separate bowl.

5. When the potatoes are cooked, peel and pass through a mouli (or use a potato masher or ricer) into a bowl. Add the spinach and bean mixture, the Parmesan cheese, egg yolks, 1 tablespoon salt, pepper and nutmeg.

6. Beat the egg whites in a separate bowl until stiff and set aside.

7. Form the vegetable mixture into croquettes, each about the size of a date. Roll each croquette in the flour, then in the egg whites, and then in the breadcrumbs. Fry in oil until golden brown, turning over once. Drain on absorbent paper and serve with cherry tomato sauce on the side.

to make the sauce:

1. Mix the garlic, basil and parsley together to form a homogeneous mix. Add the whole chilli pepper, if desired.

2. Heat the olive oil in a saucepan and sauté the herb mixture for 1–2 minutes.

3. Add the tomatoes and salt, and cook for 15 minutes until most of the water from the tomatoes is absorbed, stirring frequently to avoid sticking. Serve warm.

Maria Pia's tip: If cherry tomatoes are not available, substitute with 1 x 450g can tomatoes.

Fiori di zucchini fritti
FRIED ZUCCHINI FLOWERS (gluten-free version)
SERVES 4

for the batter
3 EGG WHITES
a pinch of **SALT**
1 tablespoon **MINT**, freshly chopped
60g **POTATO FLOUR**

1 cup **PURE OLIVE OIL** for frying
20 ZUCCHINI FLOWERS

1. Mix the egg whites (without beating them) in a bowl together with the salt, mint and potato flour.

2. Heat the oil over a moderate heat for 15 minutes.

3. Remove the pistil from the zucchini flowers, dip them in the batter and fry until golden brown, turning over once. Drain on absorbent paper and serve hot.

MARIA PIA

for vegetable-lovers
CHAPTER TWO

Insalata di cipolle rosse e bianche con melanzane e patate
RED AND WHITE ONION, POTATO & AUBERGINE SALAD

During the summer I am always looking for food that is easy to prepare, tasty and clean on the palate. I was born where the summers are always long and hot. My mother never cooked in the hot evenings, but she always had this salad ready, so she could be free to do other things. I have memories of eating it with my brothers and sisters in Leuca, by the sea.

SERVES 4–6

2 firm **AUBERGINES**
1 litre of **WATER**
juice of 1 **LEMON**
400g **POTATOES** (medium-sized)
a pinch of **SALT**
2 **RED ONIONS**, finely chopped
2 **WHITE ONIONS**, finely chopped
a handful of **MINT LEAVES**, coarsely chopped
a handful of **ITALIAN PARSLEY**, finely chopped
2 tablespoons **WHITE WINE VINEGAR**
4 tablespoons **EXTRA VIRGIN OLIVE OIL**
SEA SALT and freshly ground **BLACK PEPPER** to taste

1. Peel and wash the aubergines, then boil whole for 10–13 minutes in water until they are almost soft. Remove, drain and cool. Cut into 5cm-long strips and squeeze lemon juice over them.

2. Peel, wash and slice the potatoes into 5mm-thick rounds. Boil until tender. Remove, drain and cool. Sprinkle with a pinch of salt.

3. Put the aubergines, potatoes and chopped onions in a bowl with the mint, parsley, vinegar and oil. Toss and season with salt and freshly ground black pepper. Serve at room temperature.

Maria Pia's tips: This salad is ideal for hot summer days. The onions will help your system function well because they have antiseptic (as well as digestive) properties.

I always use Italian parsley in my recipes because it tastes better than the curly-leafed variety. It is also full of iron and is a stimulant for the liver. However, it must be chopped the moment before you use it. (Italians can be a little obsessed with health, and I am no exception.)

Scarpazzon o erbazzone salato

SAVOURY SILVERBEET PIE

SERVES 8

for the pastry
450g FLOUR
a pinch of SALT
30g BUTTER, at room temperature
2 tablespoons EXTRA VIRGIN OLIVE OIL, plus 1 tablespoon for brushing
200ml WATER

for the filling
1kg SILVERBEET LEAVES
1 RED ONION, finely chopped
2 cloves GARLIC, finely chopped or crushed in a garlic press
1 tablespoon PARSLEY, finely chopped
50g BUTTER
100g PANCETTA or BACON, cubed
150g PARMESAN CHEESE, freshly grated
300g RICOTTA CHEESE
a pinch of NUTMEG
SALT and freshly ground BLACK PEPPER to taste

MARIA PIA

to make the pastry:

1. Make a mound with the flour on a baking board and sprinkle with salt. Form a crater in the centre and add the butter, olive oil and water. Mix well. Form a ball and knead for 10 minutes.

2. Divide the dough into two unequal-sized balls for the lower and upper crusts. Cover the balls with plastic wrap and set aside for 10 minutes.

to make the filling:

1. Strip the leaves from the silverbeet stalks and wash thoroughly. Place leaves in a saucepan with a little water and cook for 5 minutes or until the leaves become tender. Drain and place on a clean tea towel. Roll tightly to wring out all the excess water.

2. Mix the onion, garlic and parsley together and set aside 1 tablespoon of the mixture for the topping.

3. Heat the butter in a saucepan and sauté the onion mixture with the pancetta or bacon for 2 minutes. Add the cooked silverbeet leaves. Mix together and cook for 5 minutes, then remove from the heat and set aside to cool.

4. In a separate bowl, mix the Parmesan cheese, ricotta, nutmeg, salt and freshly ground black pepper together and add to the vegetable mixture.

to assemble the pie:

1. Preheat the oven to 180°C. Butter a 26cm round pie dish. Roll the pastry balls into two rounds, one slightly larger than the other to cover the pie base with a 2cm overhang.

2. Centre the pastry base over the pie dish and gently press down with your fingers before adding the filling.

3. Cover with the second pastry round, folding the lower part over the upper edge and pressing down. Brush with a mixture of olive oil and water and perforate top with a fork.

4. Sprinkle with the remaining tablespoon of chopped onion, garlic and parsley. Bake for 40–50 minutes until the surface is golden brown. Serve either hot or cold, with a glass of good Lambrusco.

Maria Pia's tip: Spinach can be used instead of silverbeet, if you prefer.

Tortino di patate e cavolo nero

VEGETABLE PIE WITH POTATOES & BLACK CABBAGE

SERVES 8

650g CAVOLO NERO or SAVOY CABBAGE LEAVES
2 tablespoons SALT
700g (about 8 medium-sized) POTATOES
1 tablespoon WHITE WINE VINEGAR
4 tablespoons BUTTER
SALT to taste
500g TALEGGIO or GORGONZOLA CHEESE
freshly ground BLACK PEPPER to taste

1. Blanch the whole cabbage leaves in boiling water with 1 tablespoon of salt. Allow to drain.

2. Peel the potatoes and cut into 5mm-thick rounds. Lightly boil for approximately 7 minutes in a large saucepan of water with 1 tablespoon of salt and 1 teaspoon of vinegar. Be careful not to overcook them; they should remain al dente. Drain and spread to dry on a clean tea towel or absorbent paper.

3. Preheat the oven to 250°C. Butter a large baking tray and cover with the potato slices. Dot slices with butter and bake until they become crisp and golden. Remove from the oven and sprinkle with salt to taste. Lower heat to 180°C.

4. Butter an ovenproof dish and place half the cabbage leaves in the baking dish, covering both the bottom and the sides. Leave a good 15cm of leaves over the edge of the dish, as these will later be folded back in towards the centre.

5. Layer half the baked-potato slices and half the cheese. Repeat with another layer of cabbage, potatoes and cheese. Fold the cabbage leaves inwards so as to cover the centre of the dish. Bake vegetable pie at 180°C for 20 minutes and serve hot with some freshly ground black pepper.

MARIA PIA

Fagiolini dell'occhio al pomodoro
BLACK-EYED BEANS WITH TOMATO SAUCE

SERVES 6

500g dried BLACK-EYED BEANS

1 medium-sized ONION, chopped

1 SHALLOT, chopped

3 cloves GARLIC, chopped

1 stalk CELERY, sliced

1 tablespoon ITALIAN PARSLEY, finely chopped

1 tablespoon THYME, finely chopped

7 tablespoons OLIVE OIL

3 BAY LEAVES

1 cup TOMATO PASTA SAUCE

SALT and freshly ground BLACK PEPPER to taste

1. Soak the beans overnight in cold water.

2. Strain beans, place in a saucepan, cover with fresh water and cook without salt for 1 hour. Add more water, if necessary; the beans should always be covered with water while cooking.

3. Sauté the onion, shallot, garlic, celery, parsley and thyme in the olive oil. Add the bay leaves.

4. Strain the beans, conserving some of the cooking water.

5. Add the beans and tomato pasta sauce to the onion mixture. Cook for another 30 minutes, adding a little of the cooking water from the beans, if necessary.

6. Season with salt and freshly ground black pepper.

Zucchine in agretto
ZUCCHINI WITH TOMATOES

SERVES 4–6

500g zucchini

4 ripe TOMATOES

1 tablespoon HONEY (not overly aromatic)

6 tablespoons lukewarm WATER

2 RED ONIONS, thinly sliced

6 tablespoons EXTRA-VIRGIN OLIVE OIL

SALT and freshly ground BLACK PEPPER to taste

1 tablespoon ITALIAN PARSLEY, finely chopped

1 tablespoon MINT, finely chopped

juice of 1 LEMON

1. Wash and dry the zucchini. Slice in half lengthways and then into 3cm pieces.

2. Peel the tomatoes by submerging in boiling water for 1 minute. Remove seeds and chop.

3. Dilute the honey in the water.

4. Lightly sauté the onions in olive oil. Add the zucchini, season with salt and freshly ground black pepper and cook for 2–3 minutes.

5. Add the tomatoes and the honey mixture, cover and simmer for 10 minutes.

6. Just before the zucchini are soft, add the parsley, mint and lemon juice.

7. Cook for 1 minute further and serve.

MARIA PIA

Zucchine in carpione
SWEET & SOUR ZUCCHINI

This is an ideal dish to serve as an accompaniment for meat. It can be eaten immediately but is even more enjoyable if left to marinate for a few days. It is a favourite with diners in my *trattoria*.

SERVES 6

300g GREEN ZUCCHINI

300g YELLOW ZUCCHINI or SCALOPPINI

1 cup EXTRA VIRGIN OLIVE OIL

SEA SALT

1 ONION, finely chopped

3 cloves GARLIC, finely chopped

10 whole SAGE LEAVES

5 tablespoons WHITE WINE VINEGAR

5 tablespoons VINCOTTO

3 tablespoons LEMON JUICE

3 tablespoons HONEY, melted

1. Quarter the zucchini and scaloppini first lengthways and then across the width. Heat $1/2$ cup olive oil in a frying pan and fry zucchini until golden. Transfer zucchini to a bowl and sprinkle with salt.

2. Heat the remaining $1/2$ cup of olive oil in the frying pan and sauté the onion and garlic. Add the sage leaves, white wine vinegar, Vincotto, lemon juice and honey. Cook for 5 minutes, then add the zucchini.

3. Mix well and place in a sealed container to marinate in the refrigerator for 2–3 days.

4. Serve at room temperature.

Fagiolini con pomodoro e cipolle
STRING BEANS WITH TOMATO & ONION

I call this recipe the Italian flag. It is the combination of three vegetables that make me feel very patriotic. It is a very simple recipe and I recommend serving it with barbecued meats.

SERVES 4–6

700g STRING BEANS

3 tablespoons EXTRA-VIRGIN OLIVE OIL

400g WHITE ONIONS, thinly sliced

1 tablespoon ITALIAN PARSLEY, finely chopped

1 tablespoon THYME, finely chopped

300g TOMATOES, peeled, deseeded and chopped

1 teaspoon SALT

freshly ground BLACK PEPPER

1 tablespoon BASIL, finely chopped

1. Wash the beans and leave whole. Cook beans in plenty of boiling water for 5 minutes, then strain and set aside.

2. Heat the oil in a frying pan. Add the onions, parsley and thyme, and leave to cook slowly until the onions have almost disintegrated. Add the tomatoes, boiled beans, salt, pepper and chopped basil.

3. Cover and leave to cook for 5 minutes, then serve.

MARIA PIA

Insalata di fagiolini e patate novelle
SALAD OF GREEN BEANS & NEW POTATOES

This is a typical Italian salad of cooked vegetables served at room temperature. It makes a perfect accompaniment for grilled meat or fish.

SERVES 8

1 RED ONION, thickly sliced
1 cup WHITE WINE VINEGAR
400g NEW POTATOES
600g GREEN BEANS, washed, topped and tailed
7 small, ripe CHERRY TOMATOES or other small TOMATOES

for the dressing
1 tablespoon WHOLEGRAIN MUSTARD
1 clove GARLIC, crushed or finely chopped
1 tablespoon ITALIAN PARSLEY, finely chopped
SALT and freshly ground BLACK PEPPER to taste
6 tablespoons EXTRA VIRGIN OLIVE OIL

1. Soak the onion in the vinegar for 1 hour.

2. Boil the potatoes until tender (approximately 10 minutes). Be careful that they do not disintegrate. Drain and set aside.

3. Boil the beans until tender but still al dente (approximately 5–7 minutes). Test one during cooking. When cooked to the right point, plunge in a bowl of cold water for 1 minute. Drain and add to the cooked potatoes.

4. Halve the cherry tomatoes and add to the beans and potatoes.

5. Remove the onion from the vinegar, drain on absorbent paper and add to the vegetables. Toss the vegetables in the dressing and serve.

to make the dressing:
1. Place all the ingredients, except the olive oil, in a bowl.
2. Adding the oil gradually (as you would for making mayonnaise), whisk everything together to make a thick, creamy dressing.

Peperoni rossi, gialli e verdi al pane grattuggiato
RED, YELLOW & GREEN CAPSICUM GRATIN

I learned this recipe recently from the mother of an old friend, Vincenzo Cazzato, whom I had not seen for many years. I had never eaten capsicums cooked in this way before she cooked it for me. She had learned the recipe from her aunts. It is easy to prepare ahead of time and goes well with all manner of meat and fish dishes.

SERVES 6

750g mixed CAPSICUMS

7 tablespoons EXTRA VIRGIN OLIVE OIL

2 ANCHOVIES preserved in olive oil, drained and chopped

1 clove GARLIC, crushed or finely chopped

1 tablespoon SULTANAS, soaked in water

SALT to taste

2 tablespoons WHITE WINE VINEGAR

2 tablespoons BREADCRUMBS

1 tablespoon MINT, finely chopped

1. Quarter the capsicums, discard the seeds and the white part.

2. Heat the olive oil in a large frying pan and cook the anchovies and garlic over a moderate heat for 3 minutes. Add the capsicums and cook for 5 minutes or until soft. Transfer to a serving dish and add the sultanas, salt and vinegar.

3. In the same pan, gently cook the breadcrumbs for a few minutes until crisp.

4. Sprinkle breadcrumbs over the capsicums. Add the mint and toss gently. Serve at room temperature.

Frittata di spaghetti
SPAGHETTI FRITTATA

I sometimes make this dish for my staff at the end of an intense day of work; it is one of many recipes inspired by my father. The ingredients are almost the same as his mussel dish, *Mussels alla Gregorio* (see p. 143). Using cooked spaghetti gives this frittata an interesting texture.

SERVES 6

200g SILVERBEET LEAVES
250g SPAGHETTI
6 large free-range, organic EGGS
SALT and freshly ground BLACK PEPPER
50g PECORINO or PARMESAN CHEESE, freshly grated
1 tablespoon fresh MINT, finely chopped
5 tablespoons EXTRA VIRGIN OLIVE OIL

1. Wash the silverbeet leaves and steam or cook them in very little water until tender. Drain and place on a clean tea towel. Roll tightly to wring out all the excess water. Chop finely.

2. Cook the spaghetti al dente (approximately 7 minutes) in plenty of boiling, salted water. Drain and chop into 5cm pieces.

3. Beat the eggs in a bowl with a fork. Season with salt and freshly ground black pepper. Beat in the grated cheese and mint. Add the chopped silverbeet and spaghetti and mix well.

4. Heat the oil in large non-stick frying pan over a low heat. When it is hot (but not smoking) add the mixture, cover and cook for about 5 minutes until the edges appear crisp and the liquid has been absorbed. Move the pan occasionally to prevent it from sticking. Check that the bottom of the frittata is browned before putting a large plate over the pan and flipping it.

5. Slide the frittata back into the pan, browned side up, and cook for a further 3–4 minutes. Transfer to a heated serving dish. Can be served warm or at room temperature.

Torta salata di carciofi, bietola e taleggio
ARTICHOKE, SILVERBEET & TALEGGIO-CHEESE PIE

This savoury pie keeps well for several days. It makes a delicious snack anytime of the day, and is ideal for children's school-lunch boxes.

for the filling
1kg SILVERBEET (leaves only)
12 medium-sized ARTICHOKES
juice of 1 LEMON
2 tablespoons EXTRA VIRGIN OLIVE OIL,
plus extra for brushing the tin
50g BUTTER
4 ONIONS, finely chopped
SALT and freshly ground BLACK PEPPER
30g BREADCRUMBS
4 tablespoons MILK
150g PARMESAN CHEESE, freshly grated
1 tablespoon MARJORAM, finely chopped
150g TALEGGIO CHEESE, cubed

for the dough
500g STRONG FLOUR
5 tablespoons OLIVE OIL
250ml cold WATER
a pinch of SALT

MARIA PIA

to make the filling:

1. Strip the leaves from the silverbeet stalks and discard the stalks. Wash the leaves thoroughly and place them in a saucepan with a small amount of water, and cook for 5 minutes or until the leaves become tender. When cooked, plunge in a bowl of cold water. Drain and place on a clean tea towel. Roll tightly to wring out all the excess water and chop.

2. Strip the outer leaves from each artichoke and discard. Cut off the top (the toughest part) and also discard. Then, cut the artichoke in half lengthways and remove and discard the choke (the fluffy white part present in some older artichokes). Place the artichoke halves in a bowl of water with the lemon juice. This prevents them from discolouring. Drain, dry and cut the artichokes into 8 parts.

3. In a large frying pan, combine the olive oil and butter. When the butter has melted add the artichokes and onions. Cook over a moderate heat until tender, adding a few spoonfuls of water if necessary. Add the silverbeet and season with salt and freshly ground black pepper.

4. Soak the breadcrumbs in the milk and squeeze dry.

5. Transfer the vegetable mixture to a bowl and add the Parmesan, breadcrumbs and marjoram. Adjust the seasoning to taste. Allow to cool.

to make the dough:

1. Mix the flour, olive oil, water and salt in a bowl.

2. Transfer to a work surface and knead until soft. Divide into two balls, one slightly larger than the other. Cover and leave to rest for 10 minutes at room temperature.

to assemble the pie:

1. Preheat the oven to 190°C.

2. With a rolling pin, roll out the pie base so that it is slightly larger than a 26cm round pie dish. Roll out the top to fit the dish.

3. Brush the pie dish with olive oil and line it with the dough. Press well into the base to prevent it bubbling. Add the filling. Using your fingers, distribute the filling, pushing down the pieces of taleggio cheese into the mixture.

4. Cover filling with the upper crust and press down well. Trim the edges of the pastry and brush the top with a mixture of olive oil and water. Bake for 50 minutes or until golden brown. Allow to cool and serve at room temperature.

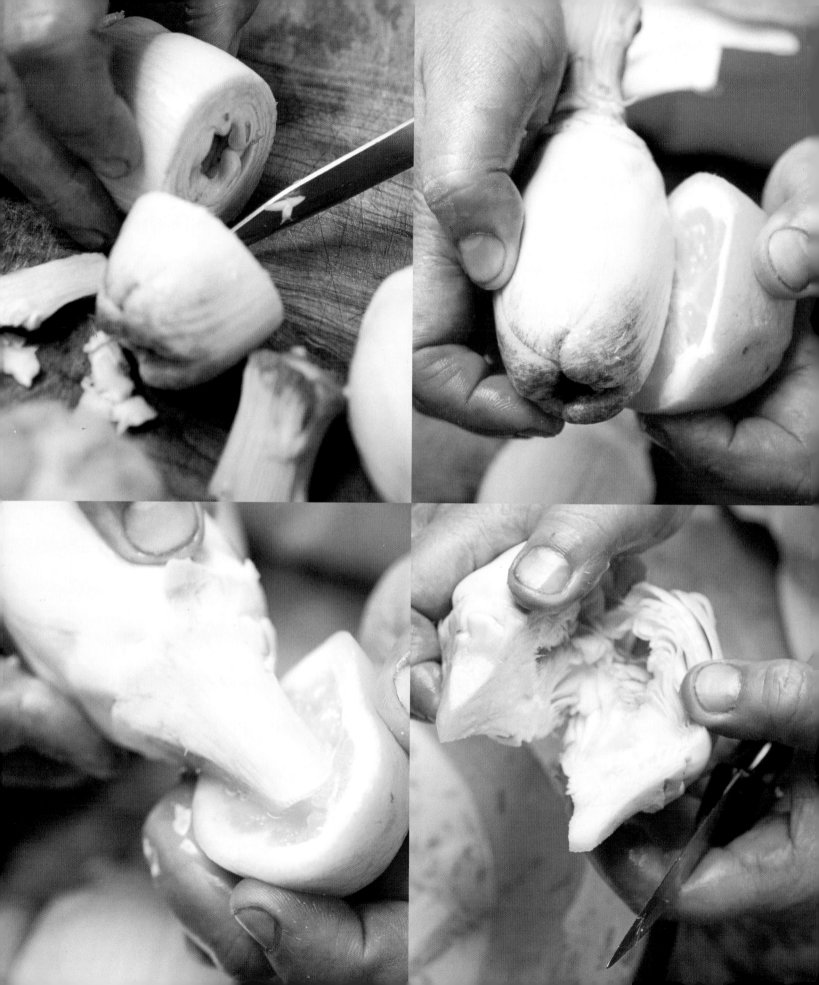

Asparagi
ASPARAGUS

Some sources maintain that the Phoenicians introduced asparagus to the Greeks and Romans. The latter cultivated asparagus as early as 200 BC. One of the first vegetables of spring, asparagus is related to onions, garlic and other plants of the lily family. There are three main types: green, white and purple, and each type comprises many different varieties.

Unless you plan to eat your asparagus immediately, it is best stored in a cool place or at the bottom of the fridge with the stems wrapped in damp absorbent paper. Fresh asparagus tastes best when cooked as little as possible, a fact apparently appreciated by the Roman emperor Augustus, who is said to have described a task done quickly as taking less time than to cook asparagus! Before steaming, boiling or grilling, snap off the tough lower stem by holding the spear in both hands and bending it from the bottom. It will break where the tender and tough parts meet.

Tinned asparagus is best avoided as it has lost all of this special vegetable's taste and texture.

MARIA PIA

Asparagi al vapore con mozzarella di bufala e salsa allo zafferano
STEAMED ASPARAGUS WITH BUFFALO MOZZARELLA & SAFFRON SAUCE

One day when cooking in my *trattoria*, I received the most gorgeous purple and pink asparagus from a grower. I literally burst into tears of joy and gave him a huge hug and a kiss – he was like Father Christmas. He said, 'I know you're the right person to appreciate this strange vegetable.' So, I quickly invented something special, and because I also receive the best-quality imported buffalo-milk mozzarella, I decided to combine the two. My customers immediately took to this dish, and it has become something that I, and they, look forward to every spring.

SERVES 4

500g ASPARAGUS (preferably mixed colours)
150g salted BUTTER
7 SAGE LEAVES, whole
a pinch each of NUTMEG, CINNAMON and BLACK PEPPER
2 tablespoons warm WATER
5g SAFFRON powder
250g BUFFALO MOZZARELLA
100g PARMESAN CHEESE, freshly grated

1. Break the tough, lower stem off each piece of asparagus. Wash and steam asparagus for 5–7 minutes, until slightly al dente.

2. At the same time, melt the butter in a double boiler and add the sage, nutmeg, cinnamon, pepper and water, whisking well to amalgamate into a sauce. Remove from the heat and whisk in the saffron.

3. Drain the asparagus and place on a warm serving dish.

4. Top asparagus with the sauce and pieces of mozzarella, and sprinkle with Parmesan cheese.

Olio piccante alla Maria Pia
MARIA PIA'S CHILLI-INFUSED OLIVE OIL

In southern Italy, we make this oil and drizzle it over pasta, soups such as *pasta e fagioli* (pasta with beans), meats, vegetables and pizzas. Unlike my mother, who preserves hot chillies in vinegar and happily eats them on bread, I am not crazy about eating chilli peppers. However, with this oil it is a different story. I prefer using dried organic chillies rather than fresh ones because the oil will last a lot longer (several months), whereas with fresh chillies it will only keep for a week or so.

MAKES 2 CUPS

7 small, dried RED CHILLI PEPPERS
2 cups EXTRA VIRGIN OLIVE OIL

1. Coarsely grind 5 of the chillis in a mortar and pestle or spice grinder. Transfer to a glass jar with a tight-fitting lid and pour in the olive oil. Cover and allow to sit overnight.

2. The following day, strain and return the oil to the jar (it should now be light pink/red in colour).

3. Add the remaining 2 whole chillies and keep covered.

4. The oil can now be used as a condiment. I recommend trying it with my *Ciceri e tria* (Lecce-style pasta with chickpeas, p. 102) and *Spaghetti aglio, olio e peperoncino* (Spaghetti with garlic, oil and chilli pepper, p. 107). I also like using it with *bruschette* – chopped tomatoes and basil on slices of grilled bread.

MARIA PIA

PIEDMONT AND ONE OF ITS MOST FAMOUS RECIPES –
Bagna Caôda

A wicked tale has it that the Piedmontese are people of very few words. This is to stop sensitive noses from smelling their breath, which, after lunch or dinner, always reeks of garlic used in copious quantities in their cooking. *Bagna Caôda* is one such dish. However, it is not just a dish for those who love garlic and strong tastes, but also for people with refined palates; the same palates that will appreciate Piedmont's high-quality red wines (and what wines!).

Piedmont is one of my favourite regions in Italy. I went there from my native Puglia, where the sea and the sultry heat are nature's protagonists, to discover for the first time the fascinating vista of the Alps and in particular the high mountainous peaks. I realised that everything that grew in that beautiful region is hidden away, unwilling to be found. You need 'know-how' to find it. Truffles are underground. Cardoons and chestnuts are prickly. The chamois is a solitary animal, and the porcini mushrooms . . . well, anyone who has ever looked for them will know what I mean.

The basis for many typical Piedmontese dishes are ingredients that ripen and are gathered in the autumn months, from September to October, when the sun has lost its vigour and the air stimulates the appetite, as well as the digestion. One summer in the 1970s, I decided to spend two months walking from one summer alpine hut to the next, along the valleys of the Alps. In the Val d'Aosta (which borders Piedmont) I discovered remote places where the best *fontina* – Aosta cheese – was produced. Every type of cheese had its own history, including *fonduta*, a dish made of melted cheese. How lucky I was to participate in those hedonistic gastronomic experiences, in the days before the mass production of food encroached upon those remote valleys!

In Piedmont everything seems to have a special flavour. In fact, even if it is a sober and robust dish, one needs to approach it first, even before picking up a fork, with well-dilated nostrils. The aromas of Piedmontese cuisine are both unmistakable and extremely varied in their fragrances. Both the cuisine and the wines are designed for true connoisseurs. How can you be indifferent to a good *Barolo*, *Barbaresco* or *Barbera* (it also has an older name, *Barbesino*) about which many ballads and songs have been written; or *Grignolino* – bright, light and young.

Piedmontese cuisine is a healthy style of food; dishes are well-cooked, but are also served with ingredients which are eaten absolutely raw for contrast, and garnished mainly with butter from the high mountain summits. The cuisine possesses a flavour of forests and small valleys in high mountains, as well as a flavour of the hills where the vines are laden with grapes . . . and under the vines – truffles! In addition to their exquisite taste, truffles have a mouth-watering aroma, which some gourmets dare to call perfume. With all due respect and admiration for this precious ingredient that mother nature gifts us, it also reminds me of something earthy and womanly (and not entirely pleasant), which for men could well be considered an aphrodisiac!

But it is the exquisite taste of the truffle that raises this ingredient out of the realms of the ordinary for me. I was lucky enough to be hosted for three days at the famous *fiera del tartufo*, or fair of the truffles, which takes place at Alba during autumn. There was in front of me a menu where each dish consisted of truffle as the sovereign ingredient. Truffle-lovers tempted by such an event should know that at Asti, which lies in the Monferrato region within Piedmont, every Sunday in October, November and the first two Sundays of December, the menus of the local *trattorie* and restaurants are dedicated to truffles. There are also a number of different village fairs and auctions dedicated to truffles that are also held in Piedmont during the autumn. My favourite fair is held in Moncalvo during late October.

The food and wine of Piedmont is exceptional – truffles, wild game, excellent wine, special vegetables, produce from hills exposed to the sun and rich plains irrigated by Piedmont's many rivers including the Po, the Italian river *par excellence*. It is an ancient, rich civilisation whose cuisine is sensational – whether you sample it in obscure eateries tucked away in remote valleys, or in farmhouses in the hills and mountains, or in the magnificent regal cities where the Italian sovereigns married into royalty from the courts of neighbouring France.

BAGNA CAÔDA

I prepared this dish for a Slow Food event in honour of garlic that my husband Richard and I held at the Ohariu Valley Hall, near Wellington, several years ago. I managed to extract this recipe from an extraordinary old woman named Rosaria Camosso, in the village of Rueglio. She was Piedmontese, but of Sardinian origin, and a photographer by trade. She guarded her recipes jealously, but in the end decided to give me this one because she recognised that, like her, I cook to give pleasure to people. One of her secrets is to soak the garlic in warm milk overnight. This neutralises the strong smell and makes it more easily digestible. I have subsequently passed on this tip to others who have cooked with me!

for the sauce
10 large cloves GARLIC
1 cup MILK
100g ITALIAN ANCHOVIES preserved in salt or oil
150g salted BUTTER
300g EXTRA VIRGIN OLIVE OIL

vegetables for dipping – cut into strips
JERUSALEM ARTICHOKES
CARDOONS (remove the fibres with a knife and soak
in cold water with a spoonful of white wine vinegar)
SAVOY CABBAGE (make sure it is firm)
CELERY
CAULIFLOWER (young, tender, white and firm)
FENNEL
RED and YELLOW CAPSICUMS
RADISHES
TURNIPS

according to the custom of the village of Pinerolo, boiled vegetables can also be used:
JERUSALEM ARTICHOKES
BEETROOT
CAULIFLOWER
POTATOES
BABY TURNIPS

MARIA PIA

to make the sauce:

1. Peel the cloves of garlic and soak them in warm milk overnight.

2. Wash the anchovies under running water. Split in half and remove the bones in one piece, along with the tail.

3. Squeeze the milk out of the garlic and chop finely (in some areas in Piedmont it is ground; in others crushed).

4. Put the garlic and butter in a thick-bottomed saucepan and cook at the lowest possible heat for 30 minutes so that it dissolves without colouring.

5. Add the olive oil and anchovy fillets, letting them simmer at a very low heat for an additional 30 minutes, stirring occasionally, until a sauce is formed.

6. *Bagna caôda* should be consumed when it is almost boiling. Serve in an earthenware or cast-iron saucepan (a fondue pot works well), kept warm by a tea-light candle.

The traditional way to serve *Bagna caôda* is in a very deep terracotta bowl with handles – the classic, unique *Bagna caôda* pot. The dish is an epicurean delight and full of conviviality, as all the guests at the table dip the vegetables into the same pot, one at a time. The vegetables (and other food) are placed on individual plates. Seated around one big, round table while you chat about everything – from the latest book you are reading to office politics, from the latest gaffe made by the president of the United States to the betrayed husband or wife – and together with a glass of Piedmont wine, it is with *Bagna caôda* that opinions and secrets slip out easily from the mouths of everyone, amidst much laughter.

It seems to me that this sort of exchange comes easily in a nation with an ancient culture that is linked to its own culinary history. People become energised through these exchanges that are both truthful and hilarious – because laughter accompanies everything, and you end up better friends than you were before.

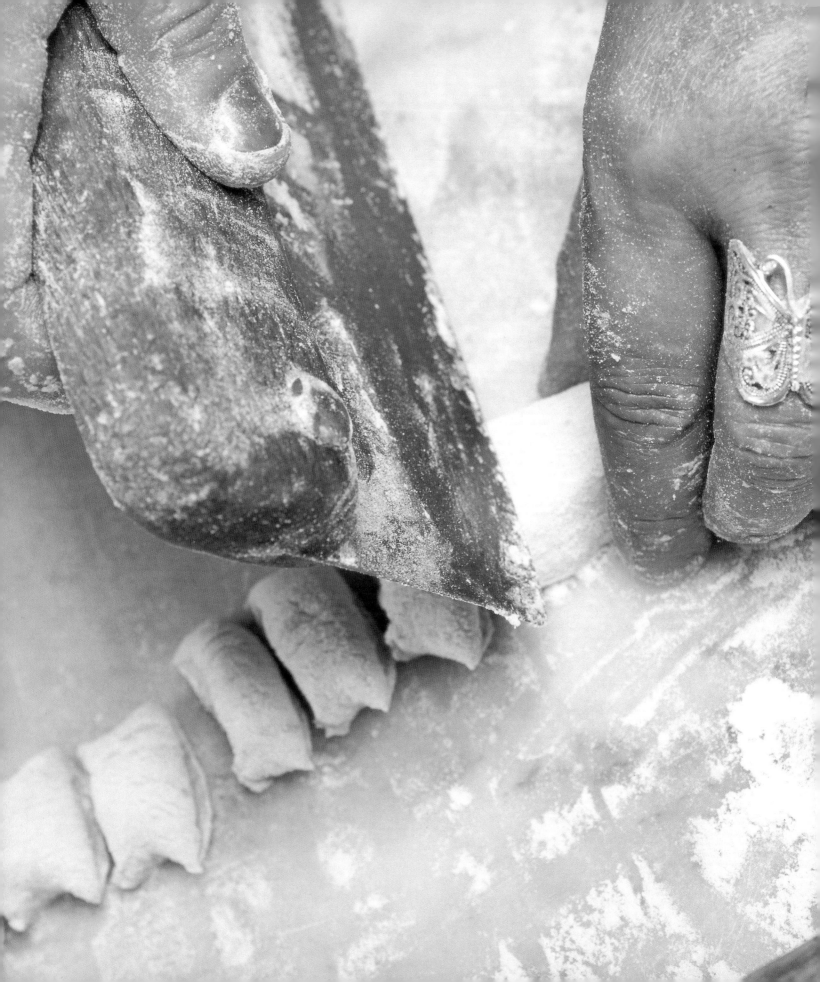

to warm the heart

CHAPTER THREE

The district of Emilia-Romagna, where I lived for well on 13 years, is considered to be among the wealthiest regions in Europe. While I was living there I taught a macrobiotic cookery course (with influences from southern Italy and Puglia) at Sant'Agata Bolognese. The course was run by the municipality who organised courses which ranged from *Tecnica come usare il mattarello emiliano* (Techniques for using the Emilian rolling pin), to English language, computers, ceramics and music. The classes were held in the library of Sant'Agata Bolognese. Carla invited me to run a series of night classes. She was a highly energetic and efficient woman, who was always turning her mind to new ways of meeting the intellectual and practical needs of the people around her.

My course was on macrobiotic sciences (from the Greek *macro* and *bíos*, meaning 'long life'). It is a form of teaching that aims for balance in body, mind and spirit through maximising psychophysical efficiencies. Philosophic and eastern religious principles are applied, in particular, to eating habits. The founder of macrobiotic sciences was Nyoiti Sokura (also known as George Oshawa). His student was Micho Kushi, who introduced it to the West, and I was lucky enough to do some cooking with his wife, Evelyne Kushi, a French woman whose open-mindedness was extraordinary. I had also studied macrobiotics in Florence at the Centro Est-Ovest di Micho Kushi, one of the few macrobiotic centres in Italy during the 1980s.

In macrobiotic cooking there are many rules to be followed in choosing and using food. Given that we all have our own biological makeup which is constantly changing at a physical, spiritual or mental level in accordance with the changing seasons, it is hardly surprising that food plays an important part in helping us maintain balance during these cycles of change. Macrobiotics fascinated me from the very start because of its strong connection with the past, present and future. I wondered what effect it would have on me, so I sought to find out. I was the ideal guinea pig.

I have to give my heartfelt thanks to Ferro Ledvinka, director of the Centre in Florence, who as well as being brilliant at diagnosis, talked with me every day about the changes that were happening to me. As his student, I was introduced to the practices of do-in, shiatsu and reflexology. I also cooked with his wife, Dominique Ledvinka, and I want to pass on some of the knowledge of food that she gave me. I lived for more than a year in their home in the middle of the Tuscan countryside. They looked after themselves and everyone around them, religiously applying the principles of macrobiotics to every aspect of their everyday lives. It was almost like a dogma for me as I rigorously monitored the signals that each season, and life in general, was sending me. I absorbed all the knowledge that surrounded me first-hand. Grasping it with my spirit, mind, heart and body was all that was required.

When I started teaching macrobiotic cookery, my daughter Dara had just turned two and Astrid, my other daughter, had started primary school. At that time we were living in the countryside, a short distance from the village of San Giovanni in Persiceto, which lies halfway between Modena and Bologna. At night, when my husband Richard came home from work and after my two daughters were in bed asleep, I would go out to teach this group of women of all ages and different backgrounds. I was attracted like a magnet to the group, and I like to think it was the same for the students. During those months we were treated to many truly unforgettable moments.

In Emilia-Romagna, the mix of southern Italian and macrobiotic cuisine that I taught was considered to be quite exotic, compared say to Chinese, Indian, even Mongolian food! In Emilia-Romagna the *dio maiale* – the divine pig – was revered; all possible food that could be derived from it was produced. Nothing could be thrown away. Everything was used, from the famous *Parma prosciutto* to *mortadella*, from crackling to bacon, from trotters to pork sausages, from *ragù* to *tortellini* – everything came from it. So, what was I doing there? I was from the South, a macrobiotic vegetarian who had grown up in the middle of olive trees up to 700 years old and whose past generations had bathed in olive oil. As Ferro Ledvinka said, this was part of my biological inheritance.

I taught these women to use pecorino instead of Parmesan cheese, and to make pasta without eggs; likewise to make *orecchiette* instead of *tagliatelle*; to use extra virgin olive oil instead of butter or lard; and to make fish dishes instead of meat, and aromatic plants and red chillies instead of black pepper. What was their response? Day by day we began to exchange our culinary knowledge and we got to know each other better. I think I loved them all — my daily life was again beginning to get richer, not only with recipes, but also through stories, faces, gestures and laughter. We related our thoughts, worries, desires, joys, and sorrows only as women (of any age or background) can when we feel we are respected and accepted for who we are, without ulterior motives.

It was at that time that I discovered the joy of bursting with laughter while cooking. These Emilian women had an innate sense of irony as a way of countering their lives — which can sometimes be hard and unjust. We would talk about nearly everything we possibly had to share, and always at breakneck speed, finishing up at midnight or later. The Emilian dialect, like all the dialects in my beautiful Italy, is like a language transformed into a song — its melody is in its gestures, cadences and expressions. Anyone listening, who understood, could also understand our attitudes towards life. I really think it is great, being Italian, to have so much diversity in our midst. Maybe we aren't the best soldiers, but this is also something to be proud of — we know how to survive with laughter and irony!

During those years I never went to the theatre or the movies, and I didn't have a television set. I had enough stories, characters and dramas; my theatre, cinema and television were right there in front of me. I didn't need a reality-television show. This period in my life also gave me time to think, as well as being a front-row participant. It was then that I decided, one day, that I would open a restaurant of my own and run it my way; not in the formal sense, where the place is manned by 'professionals'. One of my sayings at that time was: 'I am a person who lives life to the full and, consequently, everything I cook has to be full of living energy.' Destiny willed it that I eventually opened my restaurant here in Wellington in one of its most historic suburbs — Thorndon. The site is an old, character-filled house whose walls immediately began to tell me stories — stories of love, intrigue and much more.

In November 2004, I went to Italy to take part in the first Congress of Italian Restaurateurs of the World. I had the honour of representing 'Italian food from New Zealand'. I was thrilled to bits! For the first time in my life I got back some privileges from the Italian government, and without even trying! It was only through being myself, in my restaurant, and representing day after day, year after year, what I had learned from other women. I recreated their experiences gathered from cooking over the stovetops. Clearly, in the traditions of Italian cuisine so rich with history and recipes that everyone now tries to imitate, there are hundreds of years to recount and take to the table the world over. I feel the need to thank those who have contributed to this mountain of knowledge. Anonymous women, but women who live on because of the respect shown to their knowledge by people today.

Obviously, all of the trip was paid for by the Italian government — return tickets, accommodation in a five-star hotel in the centre of Rome, along with all the other 154 Italians who, like me, were there to receive their well-deserved recognition. It was like a huge saucepan used to make the best of soups — meeting people and sharing ideas, dealing with politicians and television and radio journalists — it all created a lot of intense energy.

After three days of hard work at the Congress, I felt the need to go back to Sant'Agata Bolognese to see Carla, the course organiser, whom I hadn't seen for seven years. I knew that I didn't have much time before I flew back to New Zealand, but typically (and in true headstrong Lecce fashion), if I decide something, it has to be done.

On the way, many memories of the good times I had there came back to me. Seeing each other again wasn't just a flood of tears of happiness, but much, much more. Carla reminded me of my old desire to have my own restaurant, and according to her, it couldn't help but be a success.

The recipe I want to share with you (see p. 67) which is dedicated to that experience in my life is *Passatelli in brodo* (Breadcrumb noodles in broth). This recipe was given to me by Carla's mother, who is now over 80, sprightly and full of life. She is a woman who has always worked with a belief in what she does, both for herself and others.

Passatelli in brodo
BREADCRUMB NOODLES IN BROTH

I prepared this on Christmas Day 2004 for a special guest at my home in Khandallah, Marina Mantovani, to remind her of her city, Ferrara, one of the most beautiful in Emilia-Romagna. She was almost brought to tears. Her spirit and her body were fed at the same time. This is also my daughters' favourite dish. Need I say more!

SERVES 4–6

1 MARROWBONE (big enough to produce 50g fresh beef marrow)
2 litres BEEF STOCK (see p. 68)
120g fine BREADCRUMBS
3 large free-range, organic EGGS
1 teaspoon NUTMEG
peel of 1 LEMON, finely grated
SEA SALT to taste
80g WHITE FLOUR, sifted
170g GRANA PADANO or PARMESAN CHEESE, freshly grated

1. Cover the marrowbone with water and cook until it is tender enough to remove the marrow with a spoon. When removed, set aside.

2. Bring beef stock to the boil.

3. Pass the breadcrumbs through a sieve or use a food processor to remove any larger crumbs. If making homemade breadcrumbs, use bread made only with flour, yeast and salt, and not containing oil or sugar.

4. Break the eggs into a bowl. Add the nutmeg, lemon peel and a pinch of sea salt. Beat the mixture with a fork, then add the breadcrumbs, marrow and flour.

5. Stir well until all the ingredients are perfectly blended. The mixture should have a texture slightly firmer than mashed potatoes. If the mixture is still too soft, add some more breadcrumbs. If the mixture is too firm, add a touch of beef stock. This mixture is used to make the *passatelli*.

6. To make the *passatelli* you will need a suitable tool; ideally a *ferro per passatelli* or *passatelli* press. If you don't have one, a two-handled potato masher or ricer (which looks like a large garlic press) with round holes (3–4mm in diameter) will suffice. Press the mixture down through the holes to form 3–4cm long pieces. Drop them in the boiling broth.

7. As soon as the *passatelli* come to the surface, ladle them along with a generous serving of broth into soup bowls. Top with plenty of freshly grated *grana padano* or Parmesan cheese and serve immediately. *Buon appetito!*

Brodo di carne
BEEF STOCK

Even if this is considered a classic Piedmontese dish, its traditions lie in Lombardy where meat is cooked very thoroughly, to the point where the broth becomes a *consommé*. My mother used to make this dish. She would start on Friday mornings, usually a day when we ate fish. But it was eaten on Saturdays, and sometimes Sundays, as a rich meat soup containing one form of pasta – *tortellini, pastine, stracciatelle, cappelletti* – or simply rice. Every family had its own version of *Brodo di carne*. It is perfect for warming yourself up on a cold, damp day.

SERVES 6

4 litres WATER
1/2 CHICKEN
1kg SHOULDER BEEF
1kg RUMP BEEF
1 ONION
5 CLOVES
3 stalks CELERY
1 CARROT
3 BAY LEAVES
SALT and freshly ground BLACK PEPPER to taste

1. Fill a stockpot with water and bring to the boil.

2. Rub the chicken with salt and cut off the 'parson's nose' with scissors. Wash both the meat and the chicken under running water. Place the meat and chicken in the stockpot over a medium heat. Do not use a lid at any stage of the cooking process. After about 30 minutes, skim the edges where foam has formed. Repeat this seven or eight times.

3. Stud the unpeeled onion with the cloves and add to the broth, together with the celery and carrot which can be cut or simply broken into large chunks. Add the bay leaves, salt and freshly ground black pepper. Leave to simmer over a low heat for 5–6 hours, ensuring the water never boils.

4. Set aside to cool, but do not refrigerate.

5. Take out the meat. Strain the broth three or four times. Refrigerate the broth overnight.

6. The next day, check for and remove any small hardened fragments of fat that have formed on the surface.

Maria Pia's tip: If you cook with gas, burn the onion over a flame before studding with the cloves, as this helps make a deep-coloured broth. To turn this stock into a soup, bring the broth to the boil, add pastina or rice (1/2 cup per person) and cook until al dente, taking care not to let the pasta or rice catch on the bottom of the saucepan. Sprinkle with grated Parmesan cheese and serve piping hot.

MARIA PIA

L'acquacotta
VEGETABLE SOUP

L'acquacotta is a dish I would define as a soup. For people like me who prefer not to eat a lot in the evening, this dish is ideal, especially in autumn. It is a very old recipe from Grossetano, in Tuscany, using porcini mushrooms (*Boletus edilis*). *Andare a funghi* is how you say 'mushroom gathering' in Italian. It is a sublime pleasure to cast one's eyes over a marvel such as a mushroom in a field or under a tree. It is also a moment of intense meditation … . In Emilia-Romagna, when my two daughters were little, I placed them on the seat of my bicycle, one in front and one behind. Knowing the area well and choosing the right day, off the three of us would go – to gather mushrooms. On the plains of Emilia you come across many poplars. At the end of summer, mushrooms grow abundantly on the trunks of old poplar trees that have been felled and cut. There were quite a few poplars near our house in the countryside. Carrying straw baskets and wearing leggings, my small daughters seemed like two little elves as they searched for mushrooms. And on our return, one of my favourite recipes was *L'acquacotta*.

SERVES 4–6

150g dry PORCINI MUSHROOMS
500g fresh MUSHROOMS (wild or cultivated)
1 clove GARLIC, left whole
3 tablespoons EXTRA VIRGIN OLIVE OIL
SALT and freshly ground BLACK PEPPER
250g fresh, peeled TOMATOES
1 litre boiling WATER
8 slices good-quality BREAD
3 free-range, organic EGGS
70g PARMESAN CHEESE, freshly grated

1. Soak the porcini mushrooms in water at room temperature for 1 hour. Wipe the fresh mushrooms clean with a cloth and slice thinly.

2. In a large saucepan, sauté the whole clove of garlic in olive oil. When soft, add all the mushrooms, salt and freshly ground black pepper. Cook until tender. Add the tomatoes, then the boiling water. Cook uncovered for 30 minutes on a medium heat.

3. Toast the bread in the oven and place a slice in each bowl.

4. Break the eggs into a soup tureen. Add the Parmesan cheese and beat with a fork. Add the boiling broth, cover and allow to stand for 5 minutes before ladling the broth over the bread in each bowl.

Cinestrata – ricetta antica
SOUP IN A CUP – AN ANCIENT RECIPE

This soup is one of my favourites. I was given this recipe by a family who hosted me before I went to England to visit my then-future-husband, Richard. Magda had just had a beautiful baby daughter. She taught tai chi and lived with her family in a farmhouse they were restoring in the Chianti region. The recipe probably dates from the Renaissance. Today, however, it is virtually unknown and there are very few families who make it. It is a simple and nutritious first course, especially on cold winter days. It is a great restorative for the body, and gives a burst of energy.

SERVES 6

4 EGG YOLKS (use very fresh free-range eggs)
1/2 cup dry MARSALA WINE
600ml CHICKEN BROTH, cold
a few pinches of CINNAMON
70g BUTTER, cut into small pieces
a pinch of SUGAR
a pinch of NUTMEG

1. Place the egg yolks in a bowl and add the Marsala, chicken broth and two pinches of cinnamon. Mix well and then strain into a saucepan.

2. Heat the strained mixture, adding the butter. Stir often and continue cooking until the soup thickens.

3. Pour into cups and sprinkle with a pinch each of sugar, nutmeg and cinnamon. Serve piping hot.

Zuppa alla Bolognese
BOLOGNESE SOUP

Only someone who has lived around the *Piazza Maggiore* (central square), the statue of Neptune and the market of the Jewish quarter of Bologna will be able to recall this most simple soup. Its key ingredient is *mortadella*, the emblem of a unique and inimitable salami whose real flavour is known only to a few!

A dyed-in-the-wool Bolognese, Piero Parisini, a connoisseur with a superb appreciation of the cuisine of Bologna, once paid me a compliment that meant far more to me than any Michelin star ever could. He would often receive invitations to dine at friends' homes, but systematically turned them down. These were his exact words: 'If I am at a restaurant and they bring me an unsatisfactory dish, I send it back. If, on the other hand, this dish is on a table where I am a guest, I can't refuse it. So I don't want to have unpleasant surprises. Only to your home, Maria Pia, do I accept an invitation because you know how to create the harmony of a dish to its essence.' Dear Piero, your words made me feel so proud! You are not a food critic; you are a food enthusiast and have a palate that not only recognises but also discerns the essence of love from the person who has made it. Thank you. I dedicate this recipe to you.

SERVES 4–6

80g MORTADELLA from Bologna
4 very fresh, free-range, organic EGGS
100g PARMESAN CHEESE, freshly grated
100g SEMOLINA WHEAT
a pinch of NUTMEG
SALT to taste
60g BUTTER, softened
1.2 litres BEEF STOCK (see p. 68)

1. Preheat the oven to 180°C.

2. Finely chop the mortadella. Alternatively, if you use a meat grinder, it can be put through twice.

3. Separate the eggs and set the whites aside in a separate bowl.

4. Put the egg yolks in a bowl with the Parmesan cheese and 80g of the semolina. Season with nutmeg and salt. Stir in the softened butter and the mortadella.

5. Beat the egg whites until stiff and add to the egg-yolk mix.

6. Butter a 24cm square baking tin and sprinkle with the remaining semolina. Pour in the mixture, spread evenly and bake for about 30 minutes or until a skewer inserted into the middle comes out clean. Allow to cool, then cut into small cubes.

7. Heat the stock. As soon as it starts to boil, add the cubes and let it cook for a further 5 minutes before serving.

Caciucco di ceci alla Toscana
TUSCAN-STYLE CHICKPEAS

The term *caciucco* does not have a precise origin, but in the Tuscan dialect it means *guazzabuglio* – hotchpotch. In culinary terms, it takes on the meaning of *miscuglio* or mixture. There are also meat and fish versions that are typically Tuscan. The *Caciucco di ceci* could never be accused of being a refined dish, but it is very tasty and portrays in a good light the real characteristics of Tuscan cuisine – wonderful dishes using modest ingredients (such as chickpeas) enhanced with garnishes.

SERVES 6

400g dried CHICKPEAS (or a 50/50 mix with other BEANS, such as CANNELLINI)

300g SILVERBEET LEAVES (or SPINACH, SAVOY CABBAGE or *CAVOLO NERO*)

1 salted ANCHOVY FILLET (optional)

1/2 cup EXTRA VIRGIN OLIVE OIL

1 large RED ONION, finely chopped

1 clove GARLIC, left whole

1 tablespoon TOMATO PASTA SAUCE

180g bread CROUTONS (30g per person)

PECORINO CHEESE, freshly grated

SALT and freshly ground BLACK PEPPER to taste

1. Soak the chickpeas (and other beans if using them) overnight in a large amount of cold salted water.

2. Trim the silverbeet leaves (or spinach or cabbage) from the stalks, wash the leaves and place them in a saucepan with a small amount of water. Cover and cook until tender.

3. Rinse the anchovy fillet, if using it, under running water and remove the bones and tail. Chop finely.

4. Pour the oil into a casserole dish and fry the onion, the whole clove of garlic and anchovy fillet. With a fork, reduce the anchovy to a pulp then pour in the drained chickpeas and add the silverbeet. Cover all the ingredients with cold or lukewarm water and add tomato pasta sauce. Cover the casserole and simmer slowly for 4 hours, ensuring the lid is never raised. The chickpeas should remain covered by a 2cm layer of water.

5. Slice and toast the bread croutons in the oven (or fry in olive oil if you prefer). Place some croutons in a reasonably deep plate, then ladle on the chickpeas along with some broth. Sprinkle generously with grated pecorino, salt and freshly ground black pepper and serve immediately.

Gnocchetti di pane in zuppa di spinaci
BREADCRUMB DUMPLINGS IN SPINACH SAUCE

SERVES 6

for the dumplings
3 tablespoons BUTTER
1 tablespoon EXTRA-VIRGIN OLIVE OIL
1 large SHALLOT, finely chopped
50g PARMA HAM or BACON, finely chopped
250g white BREADCRUMBS
2 cups MILK
1 free-range, organic EGG
50g WHITE FLOUR, plus a little extra for the rolling board
SALT and freshly ground BLACK PEPPER to taste
35g PINE NUTS

for the sauce
6 SHALLOTS, finely chopped
1 tablespoon EXTRA VIRGIN OLIVE OIL
350g SPINACH, washed and chopped
800ml VEGETABLE STOCK
SALT and freshly ground BLACK PEPPER to taste
PARMESAN CHEESE, freshly grated, to serve

to make the dumplings:

1. Melt 1 tablespoon each of butter and oil in a pan and sauté the shallot and Parma ham or bacon. Remove from the heat and allow to cool.

2. Soak the breadcrumbs in milk (at room temperature), then squeeze, using your hands, to remove as much of the milk as possible.

3. Place the breadcrumbs in a bowl and mix in the egg, cooked shallot, Parma ham (or bacon) and flour. Season with salt and freshly ground black pepper.

4. Transfer the mixture on to a floured surface and knead until firm enough for shaping into long, finger-thick cylinders. Slice into 2cm lengths. These are the *gnocchetti*.

5. Cook the *gnocchetti* in salted boiling water and remove with a slotted spoon once they come to the surface. Transfer to an ovenproof dish with 2 tablespoons of butter and the pine nuts. Cover and keep warm in the bottom part of the oven.

6. Make the sauce (see below).

7. Remove the dumplings from the oven and distribute into six deep serving plates. Top with steaming sauce and some grated Parmesan cheese.

to make the sauce:

1. Sauté the shallots in olive oil, add the spinach and cover.

2. Reduce the heat and leave to simmer for 5 minutes.

3. Add the vegetable stock, salt and freshly ground black pepper and boil for 3 minutes.

Maria Pia's tip: For cold winter days try using cavolo nero (Tuscan black cabbage) or any other type of cabbage instead of spinach.

MARIA PIA

Gnocchi di patate bianchi e neri con salsa alle capesante
BLACK-&-WHITE POTATO *GNOCCHI* WITH SCALLOPS

SERVES 4

for the *gnocchi*
1kg POTATOES (Agria or Desirée)
250g WHITE FLOUR (approximately)
2 free-range, organic EGGS
2 tablespoons PARMESAN CHEESE, freshly grated
20g CUTTLEFISH INK
2 teaspoons SALT
a pinch of NUTMEG

for the sauce
1/2 cup EXTRA VIRGIN OLIVE OIL
1 SHALLOT, finely chopped
1 clove GARLIC
1 RED CHILLI PEPPER, whole
300g CHERRY TOMATOES, halved
2 ZUCCHINI (1 green, 1 yellow; alternately 2 SCALOPPINI), diced
10 small QUEEN SCALLOPS in their shells
1/2 cup WHITE WINE

2 tablespoons PARSLEY, finely chopped
freshly ground BLACK PEPPER to taste

to make the gnocchi:

1. Boil the whole, unpeeled potatoes until soft. Peel and mash and divide into two quantities.

2. Make a dough by mixing half of the potatoes, approximately 125g flour (the amount will depend on the moisture of the potatoes used), 1 egg, 1 tablespoon grated Parmesan cheese, the cuttlefish ink and salt. You will need to roll the dough in extra flour to keep it dry enough to handle. This dough will make the black *gnocchi*.

3. Make a dough with the other half of the potato, remaining flour, 1 egg, 1 tablespoon of Parmesan cheese and nutmeg. This dough will make the white *gnocchi*.

4. Transfer dough balls to a floured surface and roll into lengths as thick as your index finger. Cut into 2cm pieces and roll over the back of a fork with your thumb to indent the classic ribbed pattern.

5. Make the sauce (see below).

6. Cook the *gnocchi* in plenty of salted water. When they rise to the surface, remove with a slotted spoon and place on a serving plate, cover with the sauce and garnish with parsley and freshly ground black pepper. Serve immediately.

to make the sauce:

1. In a pan, heat the oil and lightly sauté the shallot and garlic for 1 minute. Add the chilli pepper, cherry tomatoes and zucchini or scaloppini and cook for 5 minutes.

2. In a large pan, poach the scallops in the white wine until they open. Leave in their shells and discard any that don't open. Season with salt and add the sauce.

Maria Pia's tip: When the gnocchi are shaped, sprinkle with some fine semolina flour before cooking to prevent them sticking together.

Risotto con zucca e pancetta
RISOTTO WITH PUMPKIN & BACON

This is a typical dish representative of the cuisine from Mantua, where pumpkin has a place of honour equal to rice. The simple yet satisfying taste is enlivened by the addition of a few aromatic herbs. A glass of good Lambrusco is a perfect match for this dish.

SERVES 4

1.5 litres BEEF or VEGETABLE STOCK

500g sweet YELLOW PUMPKIN
(or mix with zucchini and zucchini flowers)

1 ONION, chopped

6 tablespoons EXTRA VIRGIN OLIVE OIL

30g BUTTER

100g BACON, diced, plus 2 slices for garnishing

1/2 tablespoon SALT

300g CARNAROLI RICE

1/2 cup dry WHITE WINE

freshly ground BLACK PEPPER to taste

2 tablespoons PARMESAN CHEESE,
freshly grated, plus extra to serve

2 sprigs SAGE

1. Bring the stock to the boil.

2. Peel, deseed and dice the pumpkin.

3. Sauté the onion in a pan with 1 tablespoon olive oil and 15g butter. Add the diced bacon and cook for 2 minutes. Add the pumpkin and stir. Season with salt, leave uncovered and cook for 20 minutes, stirring often.

4. Add the rice and let it cook for 2 minutes, stirring, before adding the wine. When the wine evaporates, add the boiling broth, one ladle at a time. As the broth evaporates, add more. Continue cooking, stirring occasionally, for about 15 minutes until the rice is cooked al dente.

5. Season with pepper, add the grated Parmesan cheese and stir in the remaining butter. Cover and let it sit for 3 minutes.

6. In the meantime, wash and dry the sage. Heat the remaining oil, fry the sage and 2 bacon strips until they are crisp. Pour the oil used to cook the sage and bacon over the rice and stir.

7. Pour the rice into the centre of a serving plate. Garnish with the strips of bacon over the centre and the sage around the edges. Serve immediately with a generous grating of Parmesan cheese.

La Sciuscella
SALENTO DUMPLINGS IN TOMATO SAUCE

This is a really simple recipe from my little village in Puglia, Morciano di Leuca. One of my mother's old workers gave it to me last summer. I had not seen her for over ten years. She used to take care of us six children, aged three to 11 years, and also did some cooking. Her food was always simple, traditional and wonderful.

Meeting her again was an incredible moment of emotion and memory. Warm tears covered our faces as we embraced in silence. No words were needed to remind each other of all the stories of our past. We remained speechless.

Once you've visited this part of Italy you never simply come back. Rather, you rediscover its soul each time you return. It is never the same; there is always something new. Finding it is up to you. It is as if Puglia plays 'hide and go seek' with you. Or as if it is a beautiful woman who plays hard to get. You learn many things, but never discover her completely.

Our greatest heritage is the 50 million olive trees spread over 350,000 hectares. Puglia produces 44 per cent of Italy's olive oil and 12 per cent of the world's supply of this essential ingredient.

We used to eat this dish together, with thick, warm slices of our wonderful Pugliese bread so we could *fare la scarpetta* or wipe the pan with pieces of bread until it was as clean as a whistle!

SERVES 6

MARIA PIA

for the *sciuscella*
2 free-range, organic EGGS
1 tablespoon MINT, finely chopped
3 tablespoons BREADCRUMBS
3 tablespoons PECORINO CHEESE
(preferably aged), freshly grated
3 tablespoons FINE DURUM SEMOLINA
a pinch of SALT
1 tablespoon MINT, finely chopped, to serve

for the tomato sauce
1 tablespoon EXTRA VIRGIN OLIVE OIL
5 SPRING ONIONS (including the green part),
finely chopped
10 large, ripe TOMATOES
with the skin left on, cut into small pieces
7 large GREEN OLIVES (stone in)
7 small BLACK OLIVES (stone in)
1 tablespoon CAPERS IN VINEGAR, finely chopped
SALT to taste

to make the sciuscella:
1. Mix all of the ingredients for the *sciuscella* together in a bowl. Cover and keep in the refrigerator for 1 hour. In the meantime, prepare the tomato sauce (see below).

2. Using two spoons, make balls from the *sciuscella* mixture and drop in the simmering sauce. Cook over a moderate heat without stirring but gently rotating the saucepan so that the balls do not stick together. Serve warm, garnished with mint.

to make the sauce:
Put all the ingredients in a pot. Cook until the tomatoes have liquified (about 10–15 minutes).

Malfatti o strozzapreti
SPINACH DUMPLINGS

Malfatti literally means 'badly made'. In some parts of Tuscany this dish is also known as *strozzapreti* or 'priest chokers'. Forgive me, oh Lord, if I too sometimes thought about serving up some bad clergymen, but I never did! However, one day I had the idea of mixing 3g of saffron powder in half of the mixture in order to obtain two different colours in the same dish. It worked really well!

I prepared this dish when I was interviewed by Kim Hill on National Radio. She enjoyed it and I was flattered when I saw her lick her fingers. At the time I had this flash of her as a naughty little girl happily breaking the rules of etiquette taught by her mother. I could relate to that!

SERVES 6

750g fresh SPINACH, washed and drained

300g fresh RICOTTA CHEESE

1 cup plain FLOUR, plus 1 tablespoon extra for rolling

150g PARMESAN CHEESE, freshly grated

1 large EGG

a pinch of NUTMEG

SALT and freshly ground BLACK PEPPER to taste

3g SAFFRON POWDER (optional)

80g BUTTER

7 SAGE leaves

1. Boil 1 litre water in a large saucepan, add salt and cook the spinach for 10 minutes. Drain the spinach, and when cool, squeeze out the excess water with your hands and chop finely.

2. In a large bowl combine the ricotta cheese, 1 cup of the flour, half the Parmesan cheese, the egg, nutmeg, salt, pepper and the chopped spinach. Mix well with a wooden spoon. If using the saffron, divide the mixture into two parts and add the saffron to one half.

3. Melt the butter over a low heat in a medium saucepan with the sage leaves. Turn off the heat once the butter has melted and allow the sage leaves to infuse the butter.

4. In a large saucepan, bring 3 litres water to the boil and add salt to taste.

5. Roll the dumpling mixture between your floured palms to form croquettes, then roll them in the remaining flour.

6. Cook the dumplings one at a time until they rise to the surface. Remove with a slotted spoon and transfer to a serving dish. Remove sage leaves from butter then drizzle with the sage-infused butter and sprinkle with remaining Parmesan cheese.

MARIA PIA

Ris in Cagnon
TRADITIONAL MILANESE-STYLE RICE

This way of cooking rice is even more Milanese than the famous risotto. Personally, I do not like making risotto in my restaurant because I do not want to precook it, as most chefs do, in order to make it a manageable dish for *à la carte* service. *Cagnon* rice is served alongside braised meats with gravy, such as *Ossobuco*. It is *ottimo* – excellent!

SERVES 6

2 LITRES WATER

SALT to taste

400g VIALONE NANO RICE

100g BUTTER

1 clove GARLIC, left whole

3 SAGE leaves

PARMESAN CHEESE, freshly grated, to serve

1. Bring 2 litres water to the boil in a large saucepan and add salt to taste. Add the rice and cook until al dente (approximately 15 minutes).

2. In the meantime, melt the butter in a pan and add the whole clove of garlic and sage leaves. Cook over a low heat for 1–2 minutes. Remove from the heat and allow garlic and sage leaves to infuse the butter. Remove the sage and garlic before adding butter to the rice.

3. When the rice is cooked, drain well and then add the infused butter.

4. Sprinkle with a copious grating of Parmesan cheese, mix well and serve immediately.

Focaccia ripiena tirata
FILLED STRETCHED FOCACCIA
SERVES 8

for the sourdough starter
150g POTATOES, boiled and mashed
1 teaspoon fresh or dried YEAST
30g STRONG FLOUR
150ml warm WATER

for the focaccia dough
600g STRONG FLOUR, plus some extra for kneading
4 tablespoons OLIVE OIL, plus extra for brushing the tray and the top
2 teaspoons fresh or dried YEAST
50ml warm WATER
1 tablespoon SALT

for the sauce
120g tin of TOMATOES, chopped
2 cloves GARLIC, crushed
2 tablespoons OLIVE OIL
SALT and freshly ground BLACK PEPPER to taste
1 tablespoon OREGANO
200g TALEGGIO CHEESE, cut into small pieces
250g MOZZARELLA CHEESE, cut into small pieces

MARIA PIA

to make the sourdough starter:

1. Using two spoons, mix all the ingredients in a bowl then cover with plastic wrap.

2. Leave in a warm place for 2 hours (or overnight).

to make the focaccia:

1. In a large bowl, mix the sourdough starter and all the ingredients for the dough. Using your fingers, work the mixture thoroughly and form a ball.

2. Brush with olive oil and cut a cross in the centre. Cover with plastic wrap and leave to rise in a warm place for 3 hours or until the dough has doubled in size.

3. Transfer the dough to a floured surface. Using your palms and fingers, stretch the dough until it is nearly 1 metre in length and 30cm wide. Let rest for 10 minutes.

4. Make the sauce (see below).

5. Brush a 43cm x 31cm baking tin with olive oil and centre the stretched dough over it. Let rest for 5 minutes and then stretch the dough one more time.

6. Cover the centre of the dough (i.e. the size of the baking tray) with one-third of the tomato sauce and half of the two cheeses. Let rest for another 5 minutes. Fold over one side towards the centre and cover with another third of the tomato sauce and the rest of the cheeses.

7. Press with your fingers to create indentations for the sauce and then fold the other side over.

8. Cover with the remaining third of the tomato mixture.

9. Leave to rise for another 10 minutes, then brush with olive oil.

10. Preheat the oven to 220°C. Bake focaccia in the centre of the oven for 15 minutes. Turn the baking tray around (to ensure even cooking) and bake for an additional 10 minutes. Can be served warm.

To make the sauce:

Chop the tomatoes and season with the garlic, oil, salt, pepper and oregano.

Maria Pia's tip: For a non-vegetarian version, try adding some slices of fried pancetta or bacon to the filling.

Zuppa di topinambur e scampi
JERUSALEM ARTICHOKE & SCAMPI SOUP

Jerusalem artichokes (*Helianthus tuberosus*), from the Greek words *helios* (sun) and *anthos* (flower) used to grow wild in our garden in Italy. As the botanical name suggests, Jerusalem artichokes belong to the same genus as the sunflower. They are native to North America, so it was quite a surprise to find them growing in our garden. In Europe there are well over 200 varieties.

They can be cooked and used in the same manner as potatoes: boiled, steamed, fried or turned into a delightful mash. I used to cook them for my father, who was diabetic. This plant stores its carbohydrates in the form of insulin rather than sugar. Insulin is a polysaccharide or starch that is not utilised by the body for energy metabolism. However, it does provide nutrition to health-promoting bacteria in the intestinal tract. It also helps to improve blood-sugar control in diabetics. The downside is that the insulin it contains can also sometimes cause flatulence. But taken in small quantities, Jerusalem artichokes are also a great source of iron, almost on a par with meat, but without the accompanying fat content. I used to cook them in various ways, but one of my favourites has always been this soup made with scampi or shrimp.

SERVES 6

2 medium-sized ONIONS, finely chopped

2 medium-sized POTATOES, cubed

550g JERUSALEM ARTICHOKES, peeled and sliced

1 1/2 litres VEGETABLE STOCK

SALT and freshly ground BLACK PEPPER to taste

3 BAY LEAVES

200g fresh SHRIMPS, peeled and with the veins removed

3 tablespoons EXTRA VIRGIN OLIVE OIL

3 tablespoons DRY WHITE WINE

3 cloves GARLIC, finely chopped

2 tablespoons TOMATO PASTA SAUCE

1 tablespoon CORNFLOUR or CORNSTARCH

1 tablespoon cold WATER

freshly grated NUTMEG

LEMON JUICE

1 tablespoon PARSLEY, chopped

slices of HOMEMADE BREAD, toasted (ideally use Pugliese sourdough bread)

1. Place the onions, potatoes and the Jerusalem artichokes in a large saucepan. Pour over the vegetable stock and add salt, pepper and the bay leaves. Cover and bring to the boil. Cook over a medium heat until the vegetables are tender (approximately 20 minutes).

2. In the meantime, sauté the shrimps in olive oil and, when hot, add the white wine. When the wine has evaporated, add the garlic and tomato pasta sauce. Cook for 10 minutes.

3. Transfer the shrimps to the vegetable stock and cook together for an additional 10–15 minutes. Dissolve the cornflour (or cornstarch) in the cold water and stir into the soup.

4. Bring the soup to the boil, stirring occasionally, then reduce to a simmer for a few more minutes.

5. Add the nutmeg (which shouldn't cook). Season with fresh lemon juice and parsley, and serve with slices of warm, toasted bread.

Challah
TRADITIONAL JEWISH BREAD FOR THE SABBATH

This recipe comes from my beautiful mother-in-law, Marilyn (Matty) Goldberg, whom I met for the first time only a few days before I married my Richard. But it was as if we already knew each other, possibly in some other life. Words such as 'luck' or 'good fortune' cannot describe my feelings for her nor how much wisdom I have received from her. She is a person with whom it is impossible to associate bad or unpleasant memories. All those typical problems between mothers-in-law and daughters-in-law have never touched us. She loved Italy and my Italian attitude (and, trust me, sometimes I am no sweetheart!). Family has always been her first priority. I will never forget her face, so full of emotion when our first daughter, Astrid, was born. And I will also never forget the first time I entered her kitchen on my first visit to the United States. Or when I first tasted her blueberry muffins. She puts an incredible amount of love into all the food she prepares for her family and friends. Her dinner parties are always memorable. For me she is the perfect example of the natural culinary talent of love that only a good mamma can have.

As well as teaching me how to make *challah*, she also taught me how to prepare real French toast the day after. As far as I am concerned, this is the only way to make French toast; no other bread compares!

FOR 2 *CHALLAHS*

14g granular YEAST
$^1/_2$ cup lukewarm WATER
a pinch of SUGAR
$^1/_2$ cup hot WATER
1 $^1/_2$ teaspoons SALT
3–4 tablespoons SUGAR
2 tablespoons HONEY
$^1/_2$ cup VEGETABLE OIL
3 large free-range, organic EGGS, beaten
4–6 cups FLOUR (start with 4 cups
and add the extra, if needed)
EGG WASH (1 EGG YOLK and
1 tablespoon WATER mixed together)

1. In a small bowl, dissolve yeast in the first measure of water with sugar and set aside for 5 minutes to ferment.

2. Mix the hot water, salt, sugar, honey and oil together, add the beaten eggs and half the flour. Mix well using a wooden spoon or spatula. Add the yeast mixture and the rest of the flour. Mix as well as you can, then turn out on a floured board and knead for about 5 minutes.

3. Add more flour, if necessary. The dough should be elastic and shiny. Place dough in a greased bowl, cover with a tea towel and allow to rise in a warm place for about 1 hour or until doubled in size.

4. Remove dough from the bowl, divide it in half and set one half aside. Divide the remaining half into thirds and roll each third into approximately 30cm lengths, then plait the three lengths together. Place on a lightly greased baking sheet and brush with egg wash.

5. Repeat with the other half of the dough.

6. Preheat oven to 180°C. Bake *challahs* 20–30 minutes.

MariMaria Pia's tip: Raisins may be added to the dough after the eggs, if desired. For a sweet version (ideal for French Toast), sprinkle the bread with a mixture of 1 tablespoon of sugar and half a teaspoon of cinnamon before baking.

MARIA PIA

HOMEMADE RICOTTA CHEESE

While cooking at the Rudolf Steiner Kindergarten in Bologna at the beginning of the 1990s I discovered Demeter products for the first time. This trademark refers to products grown and produced according to biodynamic principles. Since then I have always preferred Demeter to other organic products on the market.

I used to prepare and cook food with the children as part of their daily curriculum. Usually it would be bread or pasta, but one day we decided to try making ricotta cheese and it was a great success.

MAKES APPROXIMATELY 400G

800ml organic MILK
1/2 teaspoon SEA SALT
1/3 cup fresh LEMON JUICE,
strained to remove pips and pulp

1. Pour the milk into a large saucepan, add the sea salt and stir with a wooden spoon. Bring to the boil over a medium heat for 10–15 minutes. Lower the heat and add the lemon juice one drop at a time, stirring constantly and always in the same direction.

2. As the milk coagulates you will see small lumps appear on the surface; these are the curds. Do not let the milk cook for more than 1 minute longer. Remove the pan from the heat, cover with a thick towel and let it sit for about 20 minutes without disturbing it. This enables larger curds to form.

3. Line a colander or a wicker basket with cheesecloth or muslin cloth and gently strain the curds and whey, being careful not to break up the curds. Allow to drain for 1 hour. If possible, tie and hang the cheesecloth over a bowl as this will result in firmer, drier ricotta.

4. Keep the ricotta refrigerated but consume fresh – preferably within several hours, as this is when it is at its best and sweetest. If you plan on using it in baking, then you should strain it once again.

more for pasta-lovers
CHAPTER FOUR

Pasta cu lu cuettu
PASTA WITH VINCOTTO

This recipe comes from a woman from San Donato, in the province of Lecce. She was sitting on her doorway working on a *tombolo,* a type of hand-made embroidered lacy place mat. I was fascinated by the way her fingers moved effortlessly to make the intricate patterns. We easily entered into a conversation and of course were soon talking about food.

She told me how there is a profound connection between the gastronomic, spiritual and religious traditions of Salento. Vincotto, she explained, being black, reminds us of mourning for the Holy Virgin. On the day known as the *Madonna Addolorata,* or Grieving Virgin Mother, it is therefore compulsory to prepare this dish.

SERVES 6

1kg DRIED PASTA (*MEZZE ZITE*
or PENNE

500g RICOTTA CHEESE, plus 100g for
sprinkling over the pasta

5 tablespoons VINCOTTO

1 tablespoon PARSLEY, finely chopped

SALT and freshly ground BLACK PEPPER to taste

1. Cook the pasta in plenty of salted water until it is al dente.

2. While the pasta is cooking, dissolve the ricotta in a bowl using a little bit of the pasta cooking water. Add the Vincotto, then mix thoroughly.

3. Drain the pasta and pour over the sauce. Sprinkle with the extra ricotta, parsley and plenty of freshly ground black pepper. Serve immediately.

ORECCHIETTE

Orecchiette or 'little ears' are almost universally known. *Orecchiette* are typically served with turnip greens or *cime di rapa* (also known as *broccoli rabe*) and can be found on menus all over the world. In Puglia we produce and consume many types of greens, from *puntarelle* – flowering chicory spears – to wild chicory gathered in the fields. My mother used to serve them cooked and seasoned with anchovies, oil and topped with toasted breadcrumbs mixed with pecorino cheese. The use of anchovies together with green vegetables is very characteristic of Pugliese cuisine.

Needless to say, at home we always preferred freshly made *orecchiette*. You start with a dough made from *farro* or spelt flour, hard-wheat semolina and water – never eggs as it is truly southern Italian pasta. It is rolled out on a marble table into logs and cut into small pieces, which are then shaped into concave discs by rolling with your fingers over the thumb of your other hand. Keeping the rough part of the dough on the convex side, you form the edge with your index finger. It takes a while to get the knack of it. I may not be able to send text messages on a mobile phone, but my thumbs are still very fast!

You can of course use dried *orecchiette*. But I recommend always using artisan-quality dried pasta – called *pasta artigianale* in Italian. *Orecchiette* mixed with *minchiareddhi*, another form which are rolled over a small wire, are mixed together and called *recchie maritate*. This is the type I prefer to cook at my *trattoria*.

Maria Pia's tip: Always use plenty of water when cooking pasta – 1 litre for every 100g of pasta. Add the salt once the water is boiling – the ratio is 10g of salt per litre of water.

MARIA PIA

Orecchiette alle cime di rapa
ORECCHIETTE WITH TURNIP GREENS

SERVES 5

1.5kg TURNIP GREENS

7 tablespoons OLIVE OIL

1 clove GARLIC, peeled and left whole

3 ANCHOVIES, chopped

1 small RED CHILLI pepper, whole

2 ripe red TOMATOES, peeled, deseeded
and chopped (or 300g tinned TOMATOES)

SALT and freshly ground
BLACK PEPPER to taste

500g *ORECCHIETTE*

30g BREADCRUMBS

1 cup sharp PECORINO CHEESE,
freshly grated

1. Wash the turnip greens. Chop the stems into small pieces. Divide the flowers into small pieces and set aside. Cook the stems in boiling salted water for 5 minutes. Add the flowers and cook for 1 minute. Drain and set aside.

2. Put 4 tablespoons olive oil in a saucepan, add the garlic, anchovies and chilli pepper and cook over a low heat. Break up the anchovies using a wooden spoon. When the anchovies have dissolved, remove the chilli pepper and add the tomatoes and the cooked greens. Cook together for 10 minutes over a low heat, stirring gently to prevent the flowers from breaking. Season with salt and freshly ground black pepper.

3. Cook the *orecchiette* in boiling salted water until al dente. This can take up to 10–13 minutes, as it is a very hard variety of pasta.

4. In the meantime put the remaining 3 tablespoons oil in a frying pan and toast the breadcrumbs until golden brown. Set aside to cool, then mix with the grated pecorino cheese.

5. Drain and turn the *orecchiette* into the saucepan, tossing gently over a low heat for 1–2 minutes. Transfer to a large serving bowl or individual pasta dishes and sprinkle with the breadcrumb mixture.

Maria Pia's tip: 1.5kg broccoli may be used instead of turnip greens.

Orecchiette alla rucola
ORECCHIETTE WITH ROCKET

SERVES 4–6

100g fresh ROCKET, plus extra for garnishing

5 tablespoons OLIVE OIL

1 clove GARLIC, peeled and left whole

1 small RED CHILLI PEPPER, whole

200g ripe red TOMATOES, peeled,
deseeded and chopped

SALT to taste

500g *ORECCHIETTE*

BUFFALO MOZZARELLA for garnishing (optional)

sharp PECORINO cheese,
freshly grated

1. Wash the rocket leaves and chop roughly.

2. Place oil in a saucepan, then add the garlic, chilli pepper, tomatoes, chopped rocket and salt, and cook for 10 minutes.

3. Cook the *orecchiette* in boiling salted water until al dente. Drain and mix the *orecchiette* with the sauce.

4. Dot with pieces of buffalo mozzarella, if desired, and cover with freshly grated pecorino cheese. Garnish with whole rocket leaves and serve immediately.

Ciceri e tria
LECCE-STYLE PASTA WITH CHICKPEAS

This traditional dish from Lecce is ritually eaten every 19 March, the day of the patron saint, San Giuseppe, which is also Father's Day in Italy. One typical Pugliese habit is to fry a small quantity of the pasta in olive oil and use the fried strips to garnish the dish. This creates a wonderful contrast of textures. *Massa* or *tria* are a smaller type of *tagliatelle* typical of Lecce. I first tried making *tria* when I was three or four years old, under the supervision of my grandmother's servants whom we called our *tata*. According to food historian Barbara Santich, the word *tria* is of Greek origin. It is even claimed that *itria* is the first recorded word for 'noodle' in the Mediterranean. In dialect the dish is called *Massa cu li ciceri*, or *Ciceri e tria*, and it is sometimes also made with a type of broccolini called *mugnoli*. This is my version, which I sometimes make in my *trattoria*.

SERVES 6–8

for the *massa* or *tria* (the fresh pasta)
500g DURUM-WHEAT FLOUR
2 cups warm WATER, approximately
a pinch of SALT

for the sauce
400g CHICKPEAS
1 small piece SEAWEED (ideally KOMBU SEAWEED)
2 cups cold WATER
1 small ONION, sliced
2 stalks CELERY, chopped
1 CARROT, chopped
2 TOMATOES, peeled, deseeded and chopped
1 BAY LEAF
500g BROCCOLINI or BROCCOLI
a pinch of SALT
2 tablespoons OLIVE OIL (or chilli-infused OLIVE OIL)
freshly ground BLACK PEPPER to taste

MARIA PIA

to make the massa or tria:

1. Sieve the flour and make a mound with a crater in the centre. Add the water, mix well and shape into a ball. With your palm make a cross in the dough. (This is an old custom that I learned from my mother, who learned it from her mother – everyone from Salento who makes pasta also does this.)

2. Knead the pasta dough for 10–15 minutes or until soft and well amalgamated, then roll to 3mm thick. Gently fold two or three times over itself, then cut with a knife to make the small noodles 10mm x 5mm. Sprinkle with durum-wheat flour and leave to dry overnight, covered with a clean tea towel. This should make 600g pasta. Use 500g for boiling and 100g for frying.

to make the sauce:

1. Leave the chickpeas to soak overnight. Drain and rinse.

2. Soak the kombu seaweed in the cold water for 5 minutes.

3. Put the chickpeas in a saucepan, cover with water, then add the kombu with its water. When the water begins to boil, skim off the foam. Add the onion, celery, carrot, tomatoes and bay leaf. Leave to cook gently for 2 hours until the chickpeas are soft.

4. Wash and remove the broccolini heads from the stems. Cook the broccolini in 2 litres boiling water until al dente. Remove from water with a slotted spoon, then chop and set to one side.

5. Add salt to the water used to cook the broccolini, then cook 500g *tria* for 5 minutes or until they rise to the surface. Drain.

6. Fry the other 100g *tria* in olive oil until golden brown and set to one side together with the frying oil.

7. In a frying pan, mix the chickpeas, broccolini, cooked pasta and the oil from frying the *tria* for a few seconds over a high heat. Transfer to bowls, garnishing with the fried pasta strips and add freshly ground black pepper to taste.

Cappellacci di zucca
PUMPKIN 'OLD HATS' OR CAPPELLACCI

Ferrara is another city I heartily recommend you to visit! It is off the beaten track and takes you away from the main tourist-route cities, which seem to be getting ever-more crowded. You can sample this dish there, which is where it originally came from.

The passion for pumpkin has been around for centuries, and derives from the preference for sweet as opposed to savoury dishes. This was common practice in the Court of the Gonzagas of Mantua and the Estense family of Ferrara. It is entirely likely that the closeness of these two cities and the regular contact between their inhabitants resulted in the sharing of many customs and habits, including culinary ones. This pumpkin pasta dish is also great reheated the next day; in fact, it even seems to enhance the flavour.

SERVES 6

1kg sweet yellow PUMPKIN
1 EGG YOLK
100g PARMESAN CHEESE, grated, plus extra if needed
SALT to taste
a pinch of NUTMEG
3 tablespoons BREADCRUMBS
1 tablespoon HONEY
3 tablespoons ALMONDS, finely ground
150g BUTTER
1 sprig SAGE

for the pasta
450g FLOUR
3 free-range, organic EGGS
1 EGG YOLK

1. Preheat oven to 160°C.

2. Wash the pumpkin, remove the seeds and the coarse middle part, and cut into slices. Place pumpkin on a tray and cook for approximately 40 minutes. Test with a fork to ensure it is soft. Remove from oven and allow to cool.

3. Scoop the pulp from the skin into a bowl, add the egg yolk, Parmesan cheese, salt, nutmeg, breadcrumbs, honey and ground almonds. Stir well. If the mixture becomes too moist, add some more breadcrumbs and Parmesan cheese.

4. Make the pasta (see below).

5. To make the *cappellacci*, place a spoonful of the filling in the centre of each circle of pasta. Fold in half, press down the edges and wrap the edges around your finger to achieve the classic hat shape. Allow 8–10 *capellacci* per person.

6. Melt the butter in a saucepan with the sage over a low heat and allow to infuse for 5 minutes.

7. Bring a saucepan with plenty of salted water to the boil. Add the *cappellacci*, ensuring they do not stick together and cook for about 5 minutes. As soon as they come to the surface, place a layer of *cappellacci* in a deep dish, using a slotted spoon. Sprinkle with melted butter, sage and Parmesan cheese. Cover with another layer of *cappellacci* and again sprinkle with butter, sage and Parmesan cheese. Continue in this order until the *cappellacci* are all used. Serve immediately.

to make the pasta:
1. Make a mound with the flour and form a crater. Add the eggs and egg yolk and make a dough. Knead well until smooth, then rest for 30 minutes.
2. Roll dough with a rolling pin to form a 1mm sheet and cut into 8cm circles.

Maria Pia's tip: Other types of seasoning can be used – chopped bacon sautéed in butter; tomato pasta sauce; Bolognese ragù. In spring I also use asparagus and pancetta.

MARIA PIA

Spaghetti aglio, olio e peperoncino
SPAGHETTI WITH GARLIC, OIL & CHILLI PEPPER

The German actor Thomas Kretschmann, who plays Captain Englehorn in Peter Jackson's version of *King Kong*, spent quite a lot of time in Rome. When he discovered our *trattoria* in Wellington, he became a frequent guest. One day he asked me to prepare this simple, classical and quintessentially Italian dish. It is a perfect example of Italian 'slow/fast' food. When new garlic is in season I can honestly eat this dish twice or more a week. Thomas Kretschmann asked me to garnish his dish with a mixture of grated pecorino and chopped Italian parsley; I recommend you do the same.

SERVES 4

1/2 cup EXTRA VIRGIN OLIVE OIL

5 cloves GARLIC, peeled and left whole

1 medium-sized fresh RED CHILLI PEPPER,
halved and deseeded

1 tablespoon DRY WHITE WINE

3 litres WATER

3 tablespoons SALT, plus more to taste

500g artisan-quality SPAGHETTI

1 tablespoon PECORINO CHEESE, freshly grated

1 tablespoon ITALIAN PARSLEY, finely chopped

1. In a large cast-iron or heavy-bottomed frying pan, heat the olive oil and cloves of garlic over a low heat. Add the chilli pepper and cook slowly, stirring frequently to prevent the garlic and chilli from burning. The garlic should become golden brown. This takes around 5–7 minutes. Add a splash of white wine to deglaze the pan and stop the cooking. Remove from the heat.

2. At the same time, bring at least 3 litres water to the boil. Add the salt and then cook the spaghetti until it is al dente (approximately 7–9 minutes). The time will depend on the variety, so the best approach is to sample a strand from time to time. Be careful not to overcook the pasta.

3. Drain the spaghetti and add to the frying pan. Toss over a low heat until the pasta is well coated in oil. Garnish with pecorino cheese and parsley, and serve immediately.

for meat-lovers
CHAPTER FIVE

Polpette di Maria Pia alla Khandallah
MARIA PIA'S KHANDALLAH MEATBALLS

Khandallah is a suburb of Wellington where we live and where we opened our delicatessen and Italian takeaway in Onslow Road. I made dishes that became popular not only with the locals but also with people from all over town. My customers became fond of me and I of them, with many now coming to eat at our *trattoria* in Mulgrave Street. These customers helped me so much by giving me their support. At the time, I did the cooking myself, and did not have any money. We opened that place with nothing in our pockets! Thank you to all my customers from that period. I would like to dedicate this recipe to you, as I made meatballs so many times, and everyone loved them right from the start.

SERVES 6

for the meatballs
250g BREADCRUMBS
2 cups MILK
500g minced VEAL
500g minced BEEF
500g minced PORK
50g PECORINO CHEESE, freshly grated
3 free-range, organic EGGS
2 cloves GARLIC, chopped or crushed
1 cup ITALIAN PARSLEY, finely chopped
SALT and freshly ground BLACK PEPPER to taste
80g grated PARMESAN CHEESE, freshly grated

for the tomato sauce
1 ONION, chopped
1 1/2 cups EXTRA VIRGIN OLIVE OIL
2 litres UNCOOKED TOMATO PASTA SAUCE (in jars)
7 BASIL leaves
SALT and freshly ground BLACK PEPPER to taste

to make the meatballs:

1. Soften the breadcrumbs in the milk for 15 minute, then use your hands to wring out all the liquid.

2. Put the minced meat in a bowl, add the breadcrumbs, pecorino cheese, eggs, garlic and parsley. Season with salt and a generous amount of freshly ground black pepper. Mix the ingredients well. (I prefer to use my hands.)

3. Make the meatballs by rolling a knob of the mixture between the wet palms of your hands, forming a ball roughly the size of a walnut. Set aside while you make the sauce (below).

4. Add the meatballs to the sauce and cook on a low heat for 45 minutes to 1 hour. Every now and then, put a long wooden spoon down one side and gently stir the bottom of the saucepan to prevent any meatballs from sticking.

5. Serve topped with grated Parmesan and chunks of good bread, but please – not with pasta!

to make the sauce:

1. Fry the onion in oil, then add the tomato pasta sauce. Add 2 tablespoons water to the empty bottle, shake and add this liquid to the sauce.

2. Add the whole basil leaves, season with salt and freshly ground black pepper and bring to the boil.

ON THE SUBJECT OF MEATBALLS

I must mention Umberto Saba, a poet born in Trieste. Of Jewish blood, Umberto Saba came from a very poor family but one that was rich in love and affection; he was particularly close to his mother. When he was 20 years old, Umberto published his first collection of poetry under the pseudonym 'Saba', which in Hebrew means 'bread'. He loved his home of Trieste, a city I wholeheartedly encourage you to visit. He had a shop where he sold rare and old books, but before the outbreak of World War II he fled to Paris to escape racial persecution.

Umberto's poetry is essentially autobiographical and full of deep, psychological self-analysis. Since he lived between the two world wars, you can sense the pain of an entire generation in his work. But he was a clever man and turned this pain into a sort of anguish for the love of life and for those who surrounded him. This is why I have chosen the following passage, written in a letter to his daughter, Linuccia, in 1957, in which he sings the praises of *polpette* – meatballs:

'My Dear Linuccia

You have been away for so long now, from what was our home, that you ask me exactly what the "famous" meatballs in tomato sauce which your mother used to make, what raw materials they were made of. If I were to say they were made out of love, I wouldn't be saying anything new with that word. To tell the truth, I wouldn't know what else to add.'

Umberto Saba, *Poetry and Prose*, selected and translated with notes by Vincent Moleta, Aeolian Press, Bridgetown, 2004, p. 517.

I think that the message we must take from Umberto Saba is to hold on tightly to our traditions and values through love.

MARIA PIA

Arista di maiale in agrodolce
SWEET AND SOUR PORK LOIN

The cut of meat used in this recipe is the loin, taken from the back of the animal. The word *arista* has ancient origins. According to one legend, it was enjoyed by Greek bishops during the ecumenical council that took place in Florence in 1430, and they found it *aristos* – which means very good. It is a typical and well-known dish in Tuscan cuisine, but here is my own version in which I use some honey.

SERVES 6

2 sprigs ROSEMARY
2 sprigs SAGE
2 cloves GARLIC
1kg PORK LOIN
1 tablespoon SEA SALT
1 tablespoon freshly ground BLACK PEPPER
$^1/_2$ cup EXTRA VIRGIN OLIVE OIL
1 tablespoon HONEY (chestnut, if available)
juice of 1 small LEMON

1. Finely chop the rosemary, sage and garlic.

2. Cut a number of small slits in the meat and fill with the herb mixture. (In the Tuscan dialect this is called *pilottare*.) Rub the meat with the sea salt and black pepper. Bind the loin with white string.

3. Heat the oil in a large frying pan or casserole dish and brown the meat on all sides to seal in the juices.

4. Dissolve the honey in the lemon juice, then drizzle over the pork.

5. Cook the pork slowly until the liquid is nearly absorbed, but before it caramelises (about 40 minutes). Turn the meat several times during cooking, adding a little water to the pan, if required.

6. Remove the meat from the pan, remove the string and let it rest for a few minutes.

7. Strain the gravy and serve over the sliced meat, which should be medium-rare.

Carne alla Genovese
GENOVESE-STYLE MEAT SAUCE

This is a sauce that goes well with *Minchiareddhi Leccesi*, a typical pasta from Lecce. Although this sauce is called *Alla Genovese*, it is a style of preparation that is also common throughout southern Italy. It consists of slowly cooking beef (or rabbit, pork or lamb) with onion. It is gently simmered in a covered saucepan with a small amount of wine. There used to be shops in Lecce where merchants from Genova prepared a type of meat sauce with a large amount of onion. This recipe was accepted straight away by the population and adapted in their own kitchens. The original recipe dates from the 16th century and has survived almost intact in the Leccese tradition, but with the addition of tomato sauce. We normally serve the sauce over pasta, saving the meat for the second course, when it is sliced and served along with cooked vegetables or Pugliese-style pasta.

SERVES 6

1 x 1.5kg bolar of BEEF
50g BUTTER
1 cup EXTRA VIRGIN OLIVE OIL
1 tablespoon MARJORAM, finely chopped
3 BAY LEAVES
4 fresh TOMATOES, peeled and deseeded
500g WHITE ONIONS, finely chopped
2 cups WATER
2 cups dry white wine
SALT and freshly ground BLACK PEPPER to taste

1. Preheat the oven to 160°C.

2. Tie the beef with string and place in a casserole dish. Add the butter, oil, herbs, tomatoes, onions, water and wine. Season with salt and freshly ground black pepper. Cover with baking paper and tinfoil and cook for 3 hours, stirring occasionally to prevent the meat from sticking.

3. Serve the sauce over cooked *orecchiette* or other pasta.

Puglia is a frontier land. It plunges into the Adriatic and stretches into the Ionian Sea, with landscapes that look red and green, dotted with white country houses, castles, towers and monuments – filled with history, art and Baroque charm. It is my land, where pilgrims and crusaders passed on their way to conquer Jerusalem, then it came under control of the Hohenstaufens. The region still carries the authenticity of its past. Sometimes I feel that some recipes have all of this inside them.

Coda alla vaccinara
ROMAN-STYLE BRAISED OXTAIL

This is a popular dish from Rome. *Vaccinare* means 'to butcher' in the Roman dialect, referring specifically to the butchering of cows. This is also a 'poor dish', but it comes to you from the tables of generations and generations or Romans. *Buon appetito!*

SERVES 8

2kg OXTAIL and CHEEK (mixed)
2 tablespoons SALT
100g LARD or BUTTER, chopped
1/4 cup OLIVE OIL
1/2 cup PARSLEY, finely chopped
3 cloves GARLIC, finely chopped
1 ONION, finely chopped
1 CARROT, finely chopped
2 BAY LEAVES
SALT and freshly ground BLACK PEPPER to taste
1 1/2 cups DRY WHITE WINE
3 cups TOMATO PASTA SAUCE
500ml BEEF STOCK (see p. 68) or hot WATER

1. Cut the oxtail and cheek into pieces no larger than 4cm thick. Wash and soak in boiling water with the salt for 20 minutes. Remove and leave to dry.

2. In a flameproof casserole heat the lard (or butter) and oil. Add the chopped vegetables and bay leaves, sauté for 5 minutes then add the oxtail and cheek. Brown over a low heat until the meat changes colour.

3. Add salt and freshly ground black pepper and continue browning, adding several spoonfuls of white wine at a time. When all the wine has evaporated, add the tomato pasta sauce, beef stock or hot water. Cover and cook on a moderate heat for about 3 hours.

4. Let cool for a further 30 minutes and serve with polenta, mashed potato or rice.

Maria Pia's tip: Soaking the meat in hot, salted water makes it incredibly tender. Sometimes in winter when Savoy cabbage is available, I add half a head of chopped cabbage to the casserole and I serve the meat with organic sauerkraut.

MARIA PIA

SPECIAL DAYS IN FLORENCE

I lived in Florence for a few years when I was cooking at a restaurant called Apriti Sesamo (Open Sesame). It was situated on the far side of the Arno (*al di là dell'Arno*, as the locals say). In September 1985, I learned that I was pregnant with our first daughter. That day, I decided to celebrate the news by going to eat at the Buca di San Lorenzo, where you find the best Florentine tripe.

I learned how to prepare a special tripe dish from a truly marvellous woman, Nonnarina, who was not my grandmother but the mother-in-law of my father's Second Lieutenant during World War II in Greece. As soon as my father finished his law degree, he was sent as a Lieutenant to Greece. He had the responsibility of leading a group of soldiers, most of whom were from Tuscany. He taught them how to read and write during the time they were there, and developed a close relationship with his Second Lieutenant, Carlo Sarchi. They remained in contact after the war. I had the opportunity of meeting Carlo, together with his family, in 1969 when I finished high school and went for a holiday to Florence with my father.

That was when I fell in love with Florence and decided to remain there to continue my studies. Carlo was my guide as I got to know everything, and everyone, there. He helped me find my first room, in an apartment in Via Calzaiuoli – Shoemaker's Lane – just a few steps from the cathedral. A friend of his ran the newspaper kiosk just in front of the building where I lived. I later found out that he, on behalf of my father and Carlo, kept a close eye on my movements. (I would even go so far as to say that he spied on me!)

At that time there was nothing like the chaotic waves of tourists, students and traffic that you associate with Florence these days. Florence was a lot more intimate then – not only did everyone know everyone else by sight; they also knew about their lives. How things have changed! Sometimes I lament this. I don't recognise my Italy any longer. Everything is in such a mess today. Pollution, confusion, traffic, exorbitant prices – the whole place beats on you like a sledgehammer. Everything is readily available, but little thought is given to others or attention paid to one's neighbours or the environment.

MARIA PIA

Trippa alla Fiorentina
FLORENTINE TRIPE

In the San Lorenzo market, near the main Florence railway station, early in the morning between six and seven, railway personnel who have worked the night trains still gather there to savour what they call *lampredotto* (boiled *centopelle* or honeycomb tripe), which is eaten on a slice of Tuscan bread and seasoned with raw olive oil. This recipe is essentially the same as the one Nonnarina taught me.

SERVES 6

1kg semi-cooked HONEYCOMB TRIPE
2 stalks CELERY, chopped
1 CARROT, chopped
1 medium-sized ONION, chopped
5 BASIL LEAVES
100g BUTTER
1 cup EXTRA VIRGIN OLIVE OIL
5 cloves GARLIC, chopped
1 BAY LEAF
1/2 cup DRY WHITE WINE
50g PARMESAN CHEESE, freshly grated
500g fresh TOMATOES, peeled and deseeded
(or 1 cup TOMATO PASTA SAUCE and 1 ladleful hot BEEF STOCK)
SALT and freshly ground BLACK PEPPER to taste
1 tablespoon FENNEL seeds
1/2 litre BEEF STOCK, approximately (see p. 68)

1. Wash the tripe in plenty of water. Cut into thin strips, place in a saucepan and cook in salted boiling water for 15 minutes. Remove from the saucepan and place in a bowl of cold water.

2. Place the celery, carrot, onion and basil in a frying pan with 20g butter, olive oil, garlic and bay leaf. Sauté for 10 minutes, then add the white wine.

3. Remove the tripe from the water and strain through a colander.

4. Preheat the oven to 150°C.

5. Stir the vegetable mixture well and add the tripe, Parmesan cheese, tomatoes, salt, pepper and fennel seeds and cook on a moderate heat. Add the beef stock and cook until most of the liquid has evaporated and the tripe is tender. Pour the tripe into individual buttered ovenproof dishes, dot with butter and top with a generous amount of Parmesan cheese. Bake for 10 minutes.

Buon appetito e grazie 'Nonnarina' e grazie Firenze.

Fagiano ripieno al cartoccio
STUFFED PHEASANT IN A PARCEL

This dish is perfect for a dinner party as the flavours and aromas are trapped inside the paper parcel, and released only when it is slowly opened. This also has a great visual effect, and opening the parcel introduces an element of surprise for your guests at the table.

SERVES 4–6

1 x 1.5kg PHEASANT, with ENTRAILS

100g PANCETTA AL PEPE (belly pork with pepper; or use streaky bacon), plus 4 slices to cover the breast

1 cup EXTRA VIRGIN OLIVE OIL

300g BEEF MINCE

1 cup full-bodied DRY RED WINE

1 large ONION, finely chopped

2 stalks CELERY

1 clove GARLIC, finely chopped

SALT to taste

1 tablespoon LEMON PEPPER, plus extra for dusting

7 small CRAB APPLES, or 1 large QUINCE, or 1 large GRANNY SMITH APPLE

50g PARMESAN or PECORINO CHEESE, freshly grated

1 free-range, organic EGG

1 teaspoon THYME, chopped

1 teaspoon ground NUTMEG

4 tablespoons SWEET PAPRIKA

7 BAY LEAVES

1. Clean and dry the pheasant.

2. Stuff the pheasant (see below).

3. Preheat the oven to 180°C.

4. Line a terracotta (ceramic) roasting dish with a large piece of baking paper. Dust the paper with paprika and lemon pepper and place the bird on top.

5. Cover the breast with the remaining slices of pancetta or bacon and drizzle with olive oil and place the bay leaves in the centre.

6. Place two large pieces of baking paper over the bird, making sure it is amply covered. Brush the paper with the last of the olive oil. Wrap paper around the pheasant to make an airtight parcel. Bake for 2 hours.

to make the stuffing

1. Dice the entrails.

2. Dice the pancetta (or bacon), setting aside 4 slices to cover the breast while roasting.

3. In a large frying pan heat 2 tablespoons olive oil and fry the pancetta, then add the mince and entrails. When the meat is golden brown, add the wine and cook until evaporated.

4. Add the onion, celery and garlic, and season with salt and lemon pepper. Cook for 10 minutes, but do not stir too often. Transfer to a large bowl and let it cool.

5. Dice the apples and mix with the cheese, egg, thyme and nutmeg. Add to the meat mixture.

Pezzetti di coniglio alla Maria Pia
MARIA PIA'S BRAISED RABBIT

This recipe was applauded by an ex-cook for the Rolling Stones who came to eat at my *trattoria*, not long after it opened.

SERVES 6

200g EGGPLANT, diced into 1.5cm cubes

2 tablespoons coarse SEA SALT

2 cups OLIVE OIL for frying

300g POTATOES (not floury), peeled and sliced in rounds

1 YELLOW and 1 RED CAPSICUM

1 x 1.2–1.5kg RABBIT

1 stalk CELERY, chopped (preferably the tender CELERY HEART)

2 medium-sized ONIONS, chopped

100g pitted GREEN OLIVES, chopped

1 tablespoon CAPERS in vinegar, chopped

2 cloves GARLIC, finely chopped

5 BASIL LEAVES, finely chopped

7 MINT LEAVES, finely chopped

500ml BEEF STOCK (see p. 68)

3 cups TOMATO PASTA SAUCE

2 tablespoons HONEY

300g WHITE WINE VINEGAR

SALT and freshly ground BLACK PEPPER to taste

1. Place diced eggplant in a colander, sprinkle with the salt and allow to drain over the sink.

2. Heat the olive oil in a frying pan over a low heat. Fry the potatoes for approximately 6–8 minutes until soft, turning once during cooking. Drain on absorbent paper.

3. Cut each capsicum into 6 equal parts and remove the seeds and white part. Fry the capsicum in the oil used for the potatoes. Drain on absorbent paper.

4. Wash and dry the diced eggplant and fry in the same oil. Drain on absorbent paper.

5. Cut the rabbit into pieces at the joints (the 2 hind legs, 2 front legs and in 3–4 places along the spine). In the same frying pan, brown the rabbit to seal the meat and drain on absorbent paper.

6. Cook the celery, half the onion, the olives and capers in the same pan for 2–3 minutes.

7. Mix the garlic, basil and mint together.

8. Bring the stock to the boil.

9. Arrange the rabbit in an ovenproof casserole dish. Add the remaining onion, along with the fried vegetables, stock, tomato pasta sauce, honey, vinegar and the chopped herbs. Season with salt and freshly ground black pepper.

10. Cover the dish and cook on a low heat for 1 hour, shaking the dish occasionally to mix. Check from time to time and add more stock, if required.

Vitello tonnato– varianti su un piatto famoso

VEAL WITH TUNA SAUCE – variations on a famous dish

Coming from the very south of Italy, I used to spend my summers under a sweltering hot sun to the musical accompaniment of cicadas, crickets and birds. As soon as the sun sets and its rays diffuse, these creatures come out and sing in unison. Life slows down and everyone slows down as well, as if knowing instinctively that their very survival depends on it. How can you resist and not enjoy this beautiful summer heat?

You sit outside in the open, you rest in the shade, and you drink and drink and drink. The secret is to drink lots and eat little. But you have to eat well – food that is appropriate for the season, fresh appetisers that do not require you to light the oven or to spend too much time in preparation or cooking. *Vitello tonnato* is one such dish.

To understand this recipe it is necessary to go back in time, well before the refrigerator was invented and food was preserved in oil, salt or vinegar. In fact, *Vitello tonnato*, which combines meat and fish, is not a new thing – as some chefs of today would have us believe. They foolishly imagine that they have invented something that has actually, for hundreds of years, graced the tables of happy gourmands – in the days when food was not processed, frozen or full of preservatives.

MARIA PIA

Vitello tonnato alla Piemontese
PIEDMONTESE-STYLE VEAL WITH TUNA SAUCE

SERVES 8

1kg eye round of RUMP VEAL

6 tablespoons OLIVE OIL

200ml DRY WHITE WINE

1 BAY LEAF

1 stalk CELERY, chopped

2 cloves GARLIC, unpeeled and left whole

SEA SALT and freshly ground
BLACK PEPPER to taste

250g premium TUNA in oil

1 medium-sized ONION, finely chopped

2 tablespoons LEMON JUICE

3 ANCHOVY FILLETS, chopped

1 tablespoon CAPERS, chopped,
plus extra for garnish

2 cups MAYONNAISE (preferably homemade)

1. Preheat the oven to 180°C.

2. Tie the veal with white string to hold it together during cooking. Heat the oil in a roasting dish and brown the veal over a high heat. Moisten with white wine and remove from the stovetop.

3. Add the bay leaf, celery and cloves of garlic, and season with salt and freshly ground black pepper. Cook for 45 minutes, basting occasionally with the sauce that has formed in the roasting dish, adding a few teaspoons of water if necessary.

4. Remove from the oven, allow to cool and then place in the refrigerator.

5. Drain the tuna and pass through a mouli or food processor to achieve a creamy texture, then add the lemon juice. Add the anchovies and capers and blend again. Stir in the mayonnaise and taste, adjusting the salt as required.

6. Slice the veal thinly.

7. Spread one-third of the tuna sauce on a serving plate, followed by the sliced meat. Cover with the remaining sauce and garnish with capers.

Maria Pia's tip: Refrigerating the veal makes the meat easier to slice thinly. For this reason, I prefer to cook the meat the night before serving.

Vitello tonnato versione rapida
A FASTER VERSION OF *VITELLO TONNATO*

Here is another recipe for *Vitello tonnato* – a quick version!

SERVES 6

2 tablespoons EXTRA VIRGIN OLIVE OIL

800g VEAL

SALT and freshly ground
BLACK PEPPER to taste

1 medium-sized ONION, sliced

2–3 cloves GARLIC, unpeeled and left whole

5 SAGE leaves, chopped

120g tinned TUNA in oil, drained and lightly mashed

1 ANCHOVY FILLET

15g CAPERS in vinegar, plus extra to garnish

1/2 cup WHITE WINE

120ml MAYONNAISE

1. Preheat the oven to 250°C.

2. Heat olive oil in a pan and brown the veal on all sides. Season with salt and freshly ground black pepper. Transfer to a roasting dish and add the onion, cloves of garlic and sage. Bake for 40 minutes.

3. Remove from the oven. Add the tuna, anchovy, capers and white wine and bake for a further 20 minutes.

4. Remove from the oven once more. Take out the meat and set it aside.

5. Blend the mayonnaise together with the remaining contents of the roasting dish to obtain a smooth sauce.

6. When cool, slice the meat thinly. Spread one-third of the tuna sauce on a serving plate, followed by the sliced meat. Cover with the remaining sauce and garnish with capers.

Maria Pia's tip: Try both of these recipes and see which one you like best!

MARIA PIA

Salsiccia di cinghiale al finocchio e uva pinot nero

BRAISED WILD-BOAR SAUSAGES WITH FENNEL & PINOT-NOIR GRAPES

In southern Italy during the period of the *vendemmia* or grape harvest, which usually occurs in September and October, everyone seems so hopeful and full of expectations. I get the same feeling here in New Zealand because we sell plenty of local wine in our *trattoria*, and are always on the lookout for new wines to go with our food. Each year at harvest time, I feel compelled to celebrate by cooking some special dishes using local grapes, generously supplied by our friends and superb winemakers, Annette and Gary Voss from Voss Estate Wines in Martinborough.

Last year it was grape focaccia; this year I proposed the following recipe. I remember from my travels that this dish was made with fresh *moscato* or *muscatel* grapes. As I now live in New Zealand I had the idea to try it with pinot noir, the rising star of our national wine production.

Our homemade wild-boar sausages have always been popular ever since we opened Maria Pia's. Of course, you can also use store-bought sausages, but make sure that they contain fennel seeds and not chilli pepper, as the latter will overpower the other flavours in this dish. My husband Richard always prefers to grill the sausage over real wood coals in the traditional Italian manner. Try it!

SERVES 5

3 tablespoons EXTRA VIRGIN OLIVE OIL
1kg ITALIAN FENNEL SAUSAGES
3 cloves GARLIC, chopped
3 BAY LEAVES
5 SAGE LEAVES
1 teaspoon ROSEMARY, chopped
SALT and freshly ground BLACK PEPPER to taste
1 cup PINOT-NOIR WINE
2 cups PINOT-NOIR GRAPES
chopped PARSLEY to garnish

1. In a large frying pan, heat the oil over a medium heat. Add the sausages and garlic. Let the sausages brown without turning (approximately 3 minutes). Pierce in several places with a long toothpick or a fork to prevent them from bursting. Turn once and brown the other side.

2. Add the bay leaves, sage leaves, rosemary, salt and freshly ground black pepper and cook for another 3–4 minutes. Add the wine, taking care not to let it flame. Reduce to a low heat and allow the wine to evaporate, simmering until the sausages are tender (about 5–8 minutes). If the pan seems too dry, add a few spoonfuls of water.

3. Add the grapes, cover and cook for 2 minutes. Remove the lid and cook for an additional 5–8 minutes until the grapes are soft and warm but still whole, ensuring that there is always enough liquid in the pan. Transfer the sausages to a long serving dish and pour the sauce and grapes over the top. Garnish with chopped parsley and serve.

Dita di foglie di vita
STUFFED VINE-LEAF FINGERS

In the district of Lecce there is a special area called La Grecia Salentina or The Greece of Salento, comprising over ten villages (such as Calimera) where an archaic form of Greek is still spoken. Not surprisingly, the food also has strong Greek influences and this recipe is no exception. I learned it from a beautiful 98-year-old woman whom I heard speaking in her unmistakable dialect. It was quite hard to understand her Italian, but in the end I got there, and this recipe is the result. It was quite an honour for me. Vine leaves are available in jars from specialty food shops; I prefer the Turkish ones.

MAKES 32 PIECES

1 jar VINE LEAVES (64 leaves)
OLIVE OIL for brushing oven trays
2 LEMONS, peeled, deseeded and chopped
2 cloves GARLIC, thickly sliced
4 tablespoons MINT, finely chopped
600ml VEGETABLE STOCK
4 tablespoons TOMATO PASTA SAUCE

for the filling
340g ARBORIO RICE
450g minced CHICKEN (or a mixture of minced VEAL and BEEF or minced pure LAMB)
1 ripe TOMATO, chopped
4 tablespoons MINT, finely chopped
1 clove GARLIC, finely chopped
1 tablespoon GREEN OLIVES, finely chopped
1 tablespoon CAPERS in vinegar, finely chopped
1 teaspoon FENNEL SEEDS
1 tablespoon freshly ground BLACK PEPPER

1. Soak the vine leaves in warm water until tender (approximately 5 minutes).

2. Open the leaves and overlap two together with the shiny side facing upwards and the ribbed side facing down. Lay all the leaves out on the bench in this way, ready for the filling.

3. Parboil the rice for 3 minutes in salted water. (This is sufficient as the rice will subsequently be baked for one hour.) Drain and set aside.

4. Put all the ingredients for the filling in a bowl and mix together well. Put a heaped tablespoonful of filling in the centre of each pair of leaves. Roll from the bottom of the leaves, like a cigar, squeezing the filling tight, then fold in each side and continue rolling to make a tight cylinder.

5. Preheat the oven to 180°C.

6. Brush two rectangular oven trays (20cm x 15cm) with olive oil and arrange the stuffed vine leaves or 'fingers' on them. Place pieces of lemon and garlic between the fingers, as well as the chopped mint.

7. Mix the stock with the tomato pasta sauce and ladle over the fingers. Cover with tinfoil and bake for 1 hour.

8. Remove from the oven and allow to cool completely while covered. Serve with a green salad or as part of a mixed antipasti dish.

Ragù alla Bolognese
BOLOGNESE RAGÙ SAUCE FOR PASTA

The *ragù* of Bologna is without equal in the world. It is slow cooking at its best and represents the antithesis of 'cheffy' restaurant food. In Bologna they say *Fare il battuto e cuocere lentissimamente* – let the vegetables cook slowly, slowly, uncovered. This is the secret of this recipe. I make this dish all the time, as I consider myself part of the 'old school' of traditional Italian cuisine – and this dish is as traditional as they come! The longer you let it cook, the better it is, so don't be afraid to let the saucepan simmer on the back of the stove for an extra hour or two!

SERVES 6

50g BUTTER

4 tablespoons EXTRA VIRGIN OLIVE OIL

2 CELERY STALKS (or, preferably,
1 HEART OF CELERY), finely chopped

1/2 medium-sized CARROT, finely chopped

1 large ONION, finely chopped

60g PANCETTA or THICK BACON, diced

200g minced PORK

150g minced VEAL

100g minced CHICKEN BREAST

SALT and freshly ground
BLACK PEPPER to taste

50ml DRY RED WINE

300g TINNED TOMATOES, chopped

2 tablespoons TOMATO PASTE

2 tablespoons MILK

1. Melt the butter with the oil in a heavy-bottomed saucepan or casserole dish over a moderate heat and sauté the celery, carrot, onion and pancetta for 30 minutes. Add the three types of meat, salt and freshly ground black pepper. Do not stir until the meat changes colour. Allow to cook for 10–15 minutes.

2. Add the wine and cook until it evaporates. Then add the tinned tomatoes and tomato paste. Cover, reduce to a low heat and cook for 1 hour, stirring only occasionally. Add the milk and continue cooking for at least 30 minutes. Add more milk, as required, to ensure that the sauce does not dry out if left to cook for longer.

3. Serve with fresh spinach *tagliatelle* (ribbon noodles) or with dry pasta but, please, never on spaghetti!

MARIA PIA

for seafood-lovers
CHAPTER SIX

I ricci
KINA OR SEA URCHINS

In Puglia, the only region of Italy bathed by both the Ionian and Adriatic seas, we distinguish edible kina from non-edible kina by calling them male and female. In reality, though, they are two distinct varieties – *Arbacia lixula* (non-edible) and *Paracentrotus livichus* (edible and also sweet). We Pugliese are voracious eaters, particularly of seafood. Kina grows perfectly on our seabeds, especially the kina that feeds on *feoficee* seaweed, which makes them particularly sweet.

At certain times of the year and along some parts of the Italian coast, kina flavour changes because of the seasonal proliferation of certain types of seaweed, and at these times kina are not gathered. Fortunately, this is not the case in Puglia, where kina is eaten all year round.

The best time for gathering kina is in spring, when they have a fiery red colour with an intense iodine fragrance for which I go crazy. Some of my best memories are linked to my father, Gregorio, gathering kina, along with my brothers and sisters. We dived to the Leuca seabed with our *ranca* – this is a pole with a curved piece of iron designed to lift the kina easily from the rocks – and then we put them into a net fastened to the other end of the pole. Nowadays, fishing for kina is forbidden in the reproductive season. They are beautiful creatures with incredible colours, especially with the sunlight passing through the water reflecting on them. I liked to gather the violet coloured ones, and then the ones with subtle clear colours, and also the reddish and brown ones. They are prehistoric, holy creatures.

Another type of kina found in Puglia is called *Sphaerechinus granularis*. This is gathered for its large shell, which is dried, pulverised, mixed with olive oil and used as a remedy for some types of dermatitis.

Here in New Zealand you can find kina eggs in 200g punnets. The best time to eat them is in winter or spring, when they are sweet and have a red-orange colour.

Spaghetti con ricci di mare al pomodoro
SPAGHETTI WITH KINA & TOMATO

I sometimes use fresh *spaghetti alla chitarra* ('guitar string' spaghetti) made with five-grain flour and water. Of course, you can use dried spaghetti or linguine instead. Serve this dish with a glass of chilled dry white or rosé wine. In my *trattoria* I always match it with *Rosato del Salento*, the rosé wine made from Malvasia and Negramaro grapes for which Puglia is so famous.

SERVES 6

4 tablespoons EXTRA VIRGIN OLIVE OIL

1 medium-sized ONION, finely chopped

3 cloves GARLIC, peeled and left whole

1 RED CHILLI PEPPER, left whole

1 x 450g can CHERRY TOMATOES

3 BASIL LEAVES

3 tablespoons BLACK OLIVES, pitted and chopped

2 tablespoons CAPERS, chopped

SALT and freshly ground BLACK PEPPER to taste

800g artisan-quality SPAGHETTI

200g KINA

2 tablespoons ITALIAN PARSLEY, finely chopped

freshly ground BLACK PEPPER to serve

1. Heat the oil in a frying pan, add the onion, cloves of garlic and the whole chilli pepper. Sauté for a few seconds over a moderate heat and add the tomatoes, basil, olives, capers, salt and freshly ground black pepper. Continue cooking over a low heat for 15 minutes.

2. At the same time, cook the pasta in plenty of boiling salted water until it is al dente. Drain the pasta and add it to the pan. Add the kina and let it sit for 5 minutes.

3. Serve with a good handful of chopped parsley and freshly ground black pepper.

Sogliole alla salsa di scalogno
FLOUNDER IN SHALLOT SAUCE

In Salento, instead of shallots we use a type of onion called *spunzale*.

SERVES 4

3 SHALLOTS, peeled and quartered

4 tablespoons DRY WHITE WINE

4 tablespoons EXTRA VIRGIN OLIVE OIL

3 tablespoons VINCOTTO

4 tablespoons LEMON JUICE

20g CAPERS in vinegar

2 teaspoons MINT, freshly chopped

SALT and freshly ground BLACK PEPPER to taste

250g medium-sized NADINE POTATOES

4 SOLE FILLETS, skin on (approximately 700g)

1. Boil the shallots in the wine, reducing to 2 tablespoons of liquid (approximately 15 minutes). Transfer to a food processor, adding half the oil, the Vincotto, lemon juice, capers, mint, salt and freshly ground black pepper. Blend until smooth.

2. Peel and cut the potatoes as thinly as possible using a mandolin, grater or otherwise. Heat the remaining oil in a non-stick frying pan and fry the potatoes until golden brown on both sides.

3. Season the sole filets with salt and freshly ground pepper. Brush a pan with oil and fry skin-side down for 5–7 minutes. Turn and fry the other side for the same amount of time. Add salt and freshly ground black pepper.

4. Serve the fish on a bed of the crispy potatoes, spooning over the shallot sauce.

Trota
TROUT

When I moved to New Zealand, I was surprised to learn that its world-famous trout are not sold in the markets. In Italy, as in most of Europe, trout are farmed rather like salmon are in New Zealand. There are also several varieties, and we Italians love the pink-fleshed one known as *Trota salmonata*. At any rate, if you are lucky enough to have a trout fisherman in the family or for a friend, here are some of my favourite recipes.

I dedicate them to our great friend, partner in music and world-class fisherman, Lester Mundell, thanks to whom we had the pleasure of eating our first New Zealand trout!

Trota in crosta di miele
AROMATIC HONEY-CRUSTED TROUT

I love Vincotto and almonds – they make for a fantastic combination together with premium-quality New Zealand honey, which was also a key inspiration for this sweet and sour recipe.

SERVES 6

4 small to medium-sized TROUT, or 2 large TROUT
sprigs of ROSEMARY and THYME (enough to stuff the trout)
1 clove GARLIC, crushed
200g peeled ALMONDS, chopped
6 tablespoons AROMATIC HONEY
3 tablespoons OLIVE OIL
SALT and freshly ground BLACK PEPPER
4 tablespoons VINCOTTO
1/2 cup DRY WHITE WINE
2 tablespoons HONEY
juice of 2 LEMONS
PARSLEY, THYME and LEMON to garnish

1. Preheat the oven to 180°C.

2. Wash and pat the trout dry. Stuff the stomach cavity with rosemary, thyme, garlic, a pinch of chopped almonds and a few drops of the aromatic honey. Place the trout in an oiled ovenproof dish and cover with the remaining almonds. Drizzle with remaining aromatic honey, then season with salt and freshly ground black pepper.

3. Drizzle the Vincotto and white wine over the fish. Cook uncovered for 20 minutes or until cooked, depending on the size of the trout.

4. Mix 2 tablespoons honey and the lemon juice together and drizzle over the fish immediately before serving. Garnish with parsley, thyme and slices of lemon.

Trota del Sesia in carpione
PIEDMONTESE-STYLE TROUT

This recipe comes from Piedmont, a region rich in rivers and streams. Sesia is a tributary of the Po, the longest river in Italy where you find the most famous trout – *iridea, fario,* and the rare *marmorate. Carpione* is a way of conserving fish that stems from Roman times, where vinegar is the base ingredient. In this recipe, vinegar derived from the 'noble' Piedmont wines is used, so it is not just any old vinegar. At any rate, I recommend using premium-quality red-wine vinegar.

In the late 1970s, I often went to Val Susa and Val Scrivia to source special fabrics for a noted Italian designer for whom I had the privilege of working. We had contracts with the best cotton mills in Italy, many of which were in that area.

I have vivid memories of eating *Trota* in *carpione* in the most out-of-the-way *trattoria* in those remote valleys. I really love the taste of vinegar or lemon with big fish like trout, so this recipe is really my favourite of them all!

For New Zealand trout lovers, this recipe makes a nice change from the classic recipes using smoked trout. This is a very old recipe from lost traditions, to be cherished . . . *buon appetito*!

SERVES 4–6

4 medium-sized **TROUT**

2 tablespoons **BUTTER**

1/2 cup **OLIVE OIL**

1 litre **WHITE WINE VINEGAR**

1 litre **DRY WHITE WINE**

2 **BAY LEAVES**

1 tablespoon **SALEGGIA**
(a type of wild thyme, or use a mixture of thyme and sage)

2 **JUNIPER BERRIES**

1 small bunch **PARSLEY**, chopped

1 stalk **CELERY**, chopped

1. Wash the trout and pat dry. Melt the butter and olive oil together in a frying pan and fry the fish over a medium heat for 7–10 minutes on each side, turning once. Remove fish from the frying pan and drain on absorbent paper.

2. Put the vinegar and wine in a saucepan and bring to the boil. Add the bay leaves, saleggia and juniper berries and cook over a medium heat for 10 minutes. Leave to cool.

3. Transfer the trout to a container with a tight-fitting lid and pour over the vinegar mixture, the parsley and celery. Cover and let it sit in a cool, dry place for at least 1 day, preferably 2 or 3.

4. Serve as a main course with bread and a green salad.

for mussel-lovers
CHAPTER SEVEN

Mussels are a central part of traditional Pugliese cuisine. At Taranto, a city in Puglia situated on the Ionian Sea, a particular variety of black mussel is frequently harvested. Because of the unique habitat in which they are grown, these black mussels are prized and exported all over Europe. The mussel beds are situated in a small bay in Taranto, which is like a saltwater lake where the salt is sweetened by emissions of the so-called *citri*. These are freshwater subterranean geysers that create the ideal temperature and oxygen level for molluscs.

Cozze ripiene alla Gregorio
MY FATHER'S STUFFED MUSSELS

This recipe is named in honour of my father, Gregorio, who invented this and several other mussel recipes. My father was a lawyer who loved to make wine. He was also a businessman and dealt in grape must until the end of World War II. He adored mussels and I am sure he would have gone crazy for the New Zealand greenlipped variety. I am sure he watches me cooking from above and preparing these in his way in my *trattoria*. *Grazie, Papà*, for all your love, and also for having thought up this dish which features this most exquisite ingredient! I suggest seasoning the dish with a few drops of New Zealand's finest hot sauce – Waha Wera – made by Kaitaia Fire, and serving it with a chilled glass of *Rosato del Salento* or *Verdicchio*.

SERVES 4–6

1.5kg MUSSELS
2 tablespoons PARSLEY, finely chopped
2 tablespoons CHIVES, finely chopped
2 cloves GARLIC, chopped
2 free-range, organic EGGS
80g BREADCRUMBS
80g PECORINO CHEESE, freshly grated
SALT and freshly ground BLACK PEPPER to taste
2 TOMATOES, peeled and cut into small pieces
1 cup EXTRA VIRGIN OLIVE OIL

1. Preheat the oven to 180°C.

2. Scrape and clean the mussels under cold running water, removing any incrustations. Open the mussels either with a knife or by steaming in a saucepan for as little time as possible. Keep only the half shells containing the mussel.

3. Mix the parsley, chives and garlic together. Place the chopped mixture in a bowl and mix in the eggs, breadcrumbs, pecorino cheese, salt and freshly ground black pepper.

4. Arrange the mussels in an oven dish and spoon over some of the mixture. Add a few pieces of tomato to each mussel. Drizzle with oil and bake for 25 minutes.

Cozze arraganate alla Maria Pia
MARIA PIA'S CRUMBED MUSSELS IN THE HALF SHELL

In the Puglia dialect *arraganare* means to crumb or grate. This recipe is found with numerous variations in just about every *trattoria* in Puglia. If, like me, you adore capers and olives, these can also be added before the breadcrumbs are put in.

SERVES 6

1.5kg MUSSELS
1 cup PARSLEY, chopped
3 cloves GARLIC, chopped
2 TOMATOES, peeled, deseeded and chopped
1 tablespoon CAPERS in vinegar (optional)
2 tablespoons OLIVES, pitted and chopped (optional)
250g BREADCRUMBS
1 cup EXTRA VIRGIN OLIVE OIL
SALT and freshly ground BLACK PEPPER to taste

1. Preheat the oven to 180°C.

2. Scrape and clean the mussels under cold running water, removing any incrustations. Open the mussels either with a knife or by steaming in a saucepan for as little time as possible. Keep only the half shells containing the mussels. Arrange them in a ceramic dish or metal baking tin.

3. Mix the parsley and garlic together and sprinkle some over each mussel. Place a few pieces of tomato on each mussel, and capers and olives, if using, then top with breadcrumbs. Drizzle with olive oil and season to taste. Bake for 25 minutes until the crust is golden brown.

MARIA PIA

Passata di ceci con le cozze
CHICKPEA PURÉE WITH MUSSELS

Land and sea combine to make this renowned, beautiful side dish using chickpeas – an ingredient that features heavily in Pugliese cuisine. In this recipe, mussels find the right balance of flavours, and this balance is at the heart of the most traditional gastronomy from Lecce. This dish can be accompanied with *bruschetta*, slices of toasted bread rubbed with garlic, a pinch of salt and drizzled with some good olive oil.

SERVES 4

400g dried CHICKPEAS

3cm dried KOMBU SEAWEED

1 cup WATER

800g MUSSELS (choose small ones)

6 tablespoons EXTRA VIRGIN OLIVE OIL

1 tablespoon PARSLEY, chopped

1 sprig of MINT, chopped

1 tablespoon SPRING ONION, chopped

SALT and freshly ground
BLACK PEPPER to taste

1. Cover chickpeas with water and leave to soak overnight (at least 12 hours). Soak a piece of kombu in 1 cup water for 5 minutes.

2. Drain the chickpeas, rinse and put in a large saucepan, without salt. Add the kombu seaweed and the water it has soaked in. Bring to the boil and cook for 2 hours or until the chickpeas are soft. When the chickpeas are cooked, drain and set aside one cup for later. Pass the remaining chickpeas though a mouli or process in a food processor.

3. Scrape and clean the mussels under cold running water, removing any incrustations. Put in an uncovered saucepan on a high heat until they open, stirring them occasionally. Once opened, strain off the cooking broth for later use.

4. Heat the olive oil in a large pan over a low heat. Add the parsley, mint, spring onion, mussels and chickpea purée. Add half a cup (or more) of the mussel broth and the cup of whole chickpeas. Mix well and season with salt and freshly ground black pepper.

Maria Pia's tip: Kombu is dark seaweed from Japan that grows in deep oceans. It comes in pieces and is used in soups, as a garnish, in desserts, and to enhance the flavour of cooking in general. All types of pulses require cooking for a long time, and using kombu helps the cooking process. From my studies of macrobiotics I learned that it is one of the seaweeds that should be eaten at least once a week to obtain a good alkaline balance in our blood.

MY LOVE OF RICE

Rice was introduced into Europe from the Middle East, appearing first in Sicily during the period of Muslim domination, which began with the conquest under the Emirs Banu Kalb or Kalbiti in the 8th century. It began to be cultivated at that time and gradually found its way into Sicilian cuisine. It was, however, in Lombardy and Piedmont that rice found a completely natural habitat and thrived, to the extent that this area is now the biggest region in Italy producing and exporting rice.

My diet for years has been based on rice, lemon and olive oil, and this very diet helped me recover from an unfortunate gastronomic experience in Lancaster, England in 1986. I was married there and that is where my first daughter Astrid was born. It is also where I had my first experience of pies. I did not know what they were . . . I expected to find a filling of tomato and mozzarella (as it happens, mozzarella was unknown in England at that time). Instead, it was full of a gluey gelatine-like sauce, mixed with kidneys and innards of I don't know what! It seemed to sit heavily in my stomach for weeks. I kept eating rice to let my digestive system recover, and since then I have been very grateful to rice for its restorative value. I ate it every day, as did my daughter Astrid. She loved it so much she was given the nickname *chicco di riso* or grain of rice.

It's ironic that sometimes people misread the sign above my shop in Khandallah as Maria's Pies rather than Maria Pia's. I think of my pie experience in England whenever this happens. I do not think I will ever learn how to make one of those pies – it's better to leave that to someone else.

Outside of Italy, the use of rice in Italian dishes is usually associated with *risotto*. Personally, I find risotto heavy and difficult to digest. The recipe I give here is a traditional Pugliese dish called *tieddha* (which derives from the Latin *tegella*). It is baked in a particular type of terracotta dish called a *taieddhera*. Alternatively, you could use the same type of dish used for making *paella* or some other large, heavy-bottomed baking dish.

An important aspect of this recipe is that the ingredients are all raw and added in layers, then baked in the oven. Pugliese cooks have now introduced the dish to all the best restaurants and trattorias in the world. I believe that I have the honour of being the first to introduce it to New Zealand. I often prepare it for some of my regular customers, and for those who really appreciate good eating. It is an extremely fresh, simple and complete dish that makes the most out of one of its principal ingredients, rice.

MARIA PIA

La tieddha di Maria Pia
MARIA PIA'S *TIEDDHA*

I love this dish from the depths of my palate and my heart. Its pleasure is not just in the taste but its unusual texture. I hope you will love it as much as I do!

SERVES 8–10

2kg MUSSELS in their shells

150g BREADCRUMBS

150g PECORINO or PARMESAN CHEESE, freshly grated

1/2 cup ITALIAN PARSLEY, OREGANO and BASIL, finely chopped

3 cloves GARLIC, chopped

1 cup EXTRA VIRGIN OLIVE OIL, plus extra for brushing

1 large ONION, finely chopped

500g large RED POTATOES, peeled and thickly sliced

300g ZUCCHINI, thickly sliced

300g ARBORIO RICE

1kg ripe TOMATOES, sliced

SALT and freshly ground BLACK PEPPER to taste

1/2 litre MUSSEL BROTH (can substitute with VEGETABLE STOCK or hot WATER)

1. Scrape and clean the mussels under cold running water, removing any incrustations. Open the mussels by steaming them in a saucepan for as little time as possible. When opened, remove from the pan and set aside the broth for later.

2. Mix the breadcrumbs, grated cheese, herbs and garlic.

3. Brush a large baking dish with a little oil and begin assembling the *tieddha*, layering half the remaining ingredients, except the vegetable stock, as follows: onion, potato, zucchini, rice, mussels, tomatoes, salt, freshly ground black pepper and the breadcrumb mixture.

4. Pour half the mussel broth and 1/2 cup olive oil over the top.

5. Repeat with a second layer until all the ingredients have been used.

6. Place in an unheated oven, then turn to 200°C and cook for 90 minutes. Check every 30 minutes to ensure there is sufficient cooking liquid, adding more if necessary. After 1 hour, lower the temperature to 180°C.

7. Test the rice by pressing a few grains with a fork to ensure it is well cooked. The surface should be crisp; when served on the plate the crispy topping is mixed with the rest of the dish.

for lovers of sweets

CHAPTER EIGHT

Il miele
HONEY

For me, the fascination with honey lies in its nobility and mystery. It is produced through the extraordinary relationship between bees and flowers, which has been repeated over and over again since time immemorial.

Sweets made with honey can be stored for longer than those made with sugar. They also have a distinct aroma, which varies depending on the type used. Here is some advice on how to treat honey with the respect and sensitivity it merits:

- If your honey has crystallised, heat it gently – but not directly – by placing the jar in a bain-marie or double-boiler of hot water.
- Almost all sweets from Puglia include honey accompanied by Vincotto, lemon juice and orange. Honey is a basic foodstuff. One should eat more honey and less sugar.
- Replace sugar with honey whenever a sweetener is called for in savoury dishes. However, in proportion to its weight, honey sweetens more than sugar, so if you substitute honey for sugar in a recipe you must reduce the quantity of honey used. I recommend leaving one part sugar to prevent the dish from becoming overly aromatic or, in the case of cakes or biscuits, from becoming too hard.
- Given that honey is more liquid than sugar, you have to reduce the quantity of butter or liquid in respect to the original recipe. However, this is not necessary if the recipe contains cocoa or dried fruit.

- To enhance sweet dishes, fruit salads, and spooned desserts, you can use a mixture of honey diluted in lemon or orange juice. The proportion is one part honey to one part juice.
- To enhance savoury dishes such as roast meats or fish with honey, the proportion changes. It is one part honey to three parts juice.
- Honey melts well in all liquids, especially if they are lukewarm.

I had the good fortune to cook for children at the Waldorf or Steiner school in Bologna before my second daughter was born. Rudolf Steiner, born in Austria in 1861, was a scientist, philosopher, artist and educator. He is the founder of anthroposophy, which helps humankind in its quest for spiritual evolution.

When I visited the Anthroposophist Centre in Järna, Sweden in the summer of 1989, I was greatly touched by how much anthroposophy has to offer to so many diverse fields and disciplines, as well as in general everyday life: agriculture, healthcare and healing, architecture, economics, pedagogy, medicine, clothes, art, music, theatre, dance and, obviously, food and nutrition. It was another vision of the world that was reflected in my eyes. While cooking at the Steiner school I experimented with various dishes using honey instead of sugar. These two are my favourites:

MARIA PIA

Torta di pesche al miele
PEACHES & HONEY CAKE

SERVES 8

80g BUTTER, at room temperature, plus one tablespoon for buttering tin

150g SEMI-WHOLEMEAL FLOUR, sifted, plus 1 tablespoon for dusting

60g MUSCOVADO SUGAR, plus 1 tablespoon extra

150g aromatic New Zealand HONEY

a pinch of SALT

3 large free-range, organic EGGS

1 teaspoon NUTMEG

1 teaspoon ground CINNAMON

peel of 1 LEMON, finely grated

6 ripe PEACHES

1. Butter a 22cm baking tin and dust with flour. Preheat the oven to 180°C.

2. Beat the sugar and butter until fluffy. Heat the honey and add it to the butter mixture, stirring well with a whisk or a mixer.

3. Add the flour, salt, eggs, nutmeg, cinnamon, lemon peel and half of the peaches. Pour the mixture into the prepared baking tin.

4. Arrange the remaining peach slices in concentric circles, pressing them slightly into the mixture. Sprinkle the extra sugar over the peaches. Bake for 30 minutes.

Torta di riso al miele
RICE & HONEY CAKE

This is a great cake to eat as a sweet snack or to accompany a fruit salad.

SERVES 8

1 tablespoon BUTTER

1 tablespoon SEMOLINA FLOUR

500ml MILK

250g ARBORIO RICE

200g organic New Zealand CLOVER HONEY

1 teaspoon natural VANILLA EXTRACT

a pinch of SALT

2 tablespoons ARROWROOT

2 tablespoons MILK

4 free-range, organic EGG YOLKS

peel of 1 ORANGE, finely grated

1 teaspoon CINNAMON

1 tablespoon DEMERARA SUGAR

1. Butter a 22cm or 24cm round baking tin and dust with semolina flour. Preheat the oven to 160°C.

2. In a saucepan, bring the first measure of milk to the boil. Add the rice and half the honey, the vanilla extract and salt. Cook until the milk is completely absorbed (approximately 20 minutes), stirring frequently. Allow to cool.

3. Dissolve the arrowroot in the second measure of milk. When the rice mixture is cool, add the remainder of the honey, egg yolks, arrowroot and milk mixture, and orange peel. Mix well.

4. Spread the batter to a height of 3cm in the prepared baking tin. Mix the cinnamon and sugar together and sprinkle over the top. Bake for 25–30 minutes.

MANTUA – SBRISOLONA AND A LITTLE ART HISTORY

Mantua is worth a visit. It is a jewel (both the city and the province), especially for those who love Renaissance art but hate hordes of tourists. Of no lesser standing than the illustrious Medicis of Florence, the Gonzagas were for centuries the absolute lords of the city. They shaped it into a flourishing state on a par with any of the notable capitals of Europe. The Gonzagas took control in 1328 and ruled Mantua until 1708, when it passed into the control of Austria. It was retaken by Mantua patriots in 1868 during the *risorgimento*, the Italian movement for independence and unification.

Under the Gonzagas the development of Renaissance art was prodigious. The art of Mantua can be divided into three main periods. The first was 1450–80. It was the beginning of the transformation of the Palazzo Ducale into a sumptuous royal palace decorated with frescoes by the great masters Mantegna (the *Sala degli Sposi* or *Bridal Chamber* is a must-see), and Pisanello. The superb monumental churches of Sant'Andrea and San Sebastiano also hail from this period. The second period was 1430–1524 when the great works were completed, and the enchanting apartment of Isabella d'Este in the royal palace was adorned with the *Camera Picta* or *Painted Chamber* painted by Mantegna. The third period coincides with the arrival in 1546 of Giulio Pippi (known as Giulio Romano). One of the foremost painters in the Mannerist style, Romano completed the royal palace, turning it into one of the most spectacular buildings in the world. The Mantua Cathedral and the Tè Palace (the grandiose villa of Frederic II Gonzaga in the Tejeto area, hence the name) were also erected in this period. In the main courtyard the refined Casino della Grotta was opened, with the rich, ornate internal furnishings and decorations executed by Giulio Pippi.

La Torta sbrisolona o sbrisolada
CRUMBLY ALMOND CAKE

The ingredients for this cake are rather loosely bound in the batter. It crumbles when sliced, hence the name. To present it well, I advise slicing it in diamond shapes as soon as it comes out of the oven and while still in the baking tin. If stored in a well-sealed container, it keeps perfectly for up to a month. This cake is ideal for when unexpected guests arrive. It can be served as it is, with a good cup of tea or coffee, or perhaps a liqueur. Even better is to follow the Mantua tradition of dunking a piece of *sbrisolona* in a glass of sweet white wine, straight from the *cantina* or wine cellar. You will immediately be transported through time to the court of the mighty Gonzagas! I have always loved dry pastries and cakes, and this is one of my top favourites.

SERVES 8–10

150g BUTTER, plus extra for greasing the baking tin
125g WALNUTS
80g shelled ALMONDS
60g HAZELNUTS, peeled and toasted
100g CASTOR SUGAR
350g WHITE FLOUR
80g yellow POLENTA FLOUR
1 teaspoon BAKING POWDER
1 teaspoon natural VANILLA EXTRACT
a pinch of SALT
1 free-range, organic EGG
1 free-range, organic EGG YOLK

1. Grease a 30cm round baking tin and line with baking paper. Preheat the oven to 170°C.

2. Place the walnuts in a bowl and cover with water. Leave for at least 3 hours or, preferably, overnight – changing the water 2–3 times.

3. Drain in a colander. Set 5 almonds and 3 hazelnuts aside for decorating the cake. In a food processor, blend the remaining almonds and hazelnuts together with the walnuts and sugar for a few seconds to obtain a coarse mixture.

4. In a bowl, mix the butter and white flour, rubbing the ingredients with your hands to form pea-sized lumps. With a wooden spoon, mix in the polenta flour, chopped nuts, baking powder, vanilla, salt, egg and egg yolk.

5. Put the cake mixture in the prepared tin and, using your knuckles, press down the mixture firmly. Leave the indentations formed by your knuckles!

6. Decorate by pressing in the remaining whole almonds and hazelnuts. Bake at 170°C for 30 minutes, then increase to 220°C for a further 10 minutes to finish. Serve at room temperature.

Friteddi
RICE SWEETS

This dish is another example of how rice is a popular Mediterranean ingredient derived from contact with the Arab world. The use of fermented then fried dough is particularly common in Middle Eastern cuisine. *Friteddi* can be both savoury or sweet – the ingredients vary from potato to pumpkin to ricotta. Don't worry if the shapes all come out differently – this is intentional!

SERVES 6

400ml MILK
400ml WATER
250g VILONE NANO or ARBORIO RICE
zest of 1 ORANGE, finely grated
1 teaspoon CINNAMON
15g HONEY
50g SUGAR
70g FLOUR
5g fresh YEAST
1 litre pure OLIVE OIL for frying

1. Pour the milk and water into a pan, heat, and as soon as it starts to boil, add the rice. Cook on a low heat until all the liquid is absorbed. Transfer to a large mixing bowl and allow to cool.

2. Add the orange zest, cinnamon, honey, 30g sugar, flour and yeast. Mix thoroughly, cover with a damp tea towel and leave to rise for 1–2 hours in a warm place.

3. Heat the oil over a low heat in a deep-frying pan.

4. Drop a tablespoon of the dough at a time into the hot oil. Fry until golden brown. Drain with a slotted spoon and roll in the remaining sugar. Serve hot.

COFFEE

'Coffee should be hot as hell, black as the devil, pure as an angel and as sweet as love.' This is an Italian saying I learned when I was small and to this day I love the aroma of fresh roasting coffee. It is so evocative. Lucio Battisti was one of my favourite singers from my teenage years. In his song 'Anna' he highlights how coffee is a ritual, and also a type of protection: 'In the mornings there is someone who makes my coffee . . .' For him it is impossible to begin the day without the comfort of his beloved making that first cup of coffee.

A renowned Italian actor, Edoardo de Filippo, in one of his many theatrical roles, tells his dumbfounded servant just how important coffee is to him, as he sips on his first cup of the day: 'When I die, you bring me coffee and you will see how I will rise again, just like Lazarus!'

Then there is the legendary Toto. He was an Italian comic who, with his incredibly elastic face, performed many characters using his most Italian gift of satirical comedy, especially in the 1950s and 1960s. In a scene from one of his many films, Toto played a policeman. He turns to a waitress who has just given him an espresso over the counter – the bar is called *Caffè dello Sport* (The Sports Bar). With great solemnity, taking his first sip from the white cup, he passes his sentence: 'This is disgusting (*ciofeca*)! It isn't coffee, it's disgusting! The sign over the door shouldn't say *Caffè dello Sport*, it should say *Ciofeca dello Sport*!' This term has since become synonymous with coffee that is either too watery, burnt or otherwise undrinkable. Unfortunately, I too have also had more than my fair share of bad coffee.

However, in Wellington we are lucky to have many fine coffee roasters and suppliers. Our favourite, Coffee Supreme, supplies us with a special blend which reminds us of the aroma and taste of true Italian espresso.

Soufflé amoroso al caffè in tazzina
LOVERS' COFFEE SOUFFLÉ IN A CUP

The customers in my *trattoria* adore this curious and delicious dessert. A small glass of Sambuca is a perfect match.

SERVES 6

150ml MILK

50ml strong black COFFEE
(espresso or 'short black')

60g CASTOR SUGAR, plus 10g, and
extra to sprinkle on the cups

a pinch of CINNAMON

40g FLOUR

60g BUTTER

2 free-range, organic EGG YOLKS

3 free-range, organic EGG WHITES

a pinch of SALT

60g BITTER CHOCOLATE, in pieces

1. Preheat the oven to 200°C.

2. Butter 6 small white coffee cups and sprinkle with a little sugar.

3. Boil the milk with the coffee, 60g sugar and cinnamon, then leave to cool.

4. Thoroughly mix the flour and butter. Add the egg yolks.

5. In the meantime, beat the egg whites with 10g sugar and a pinch of salt.

6. Combine the milk with the egg yolk mixture, then carefully fold in the egg whites, ensuring they remain fluffy. Half fill the coffee cups, add a few pieces of chocolate and top off with more egg mixture. Bake for 15 minutes. Serve immediately.

Torta di tagliolini (specialità della Bassa Mantovana)
CAKE WITH *TAGLIOLINI* PASTA specialty of the Mantua lowlands

This recipe, with a few variations, is considered typical of several regions of Northern Italy, especially Emilia-Romagna. The main difference in my version is that the pasta is placed directly on the surface of the baking tin, whereas in the version from Emilia-Romagna you roll out a base before putting in the *tagliolini*.

SERVES 8

1 tablespoon BUTTER for greasing tin
1 tablespoon FLOUR for dusting tin

for the taglioni
300g WHITE FLOUR
1 free-range, organic EGG
1 free-range, organic EGG YOLK
1 cup SAMBUCA liqueur

for the cake
150g shelled ALMONDS, chopped
150g PISTACHIOS, chopped
100g WALNUTS, chopped
1 free-range, organic EGG
100g BUTTER, plus 30g
for dotting on top
300g CASTOR SUGAR
1 tablespoon natural
VANILLA EXTRACT
100g unsweetened
COCOA POWDER
50g dry AMARETTI
BISCUITS, pounded
1 EGG YOLK for brushing
1 tablespoon SAMBUCA for brushing

1. Butter and flour the base and sides of a 26cm round baking tin. Preheat the oven to 200°C.

to make the tagliolini:
1. Make a mound of the flour, form a crater and work in the egg, egg yolk and the sambuca. Knead the mixture until smooth and roll out to a thickness of 2mm. Leave to dry.
2. When dry, cut into 15cm-long strips as thinly as you can (less than a strand of spaghetti). These are known as *tagliolini*.

to prepare the cake:
1. Place the almonds, pistachios and walnuts in a bowl with the egg, butter, sugar, vanilla extract, cocoa and amaretti biscuits.
2. Spread a layer of the tagliolini over the base of the prepared baking tin and dust with a few spoonfuls of the nut mixture. Repeat the layers until all the ingredients have been used.
3. Dot the last layer with pieces of butter. Bake for 30 minutes. After the first 20 minutes of baking, mix the egg yolk with 1 tablespoon of the Sambuca and brush over the cake. Finish baking until the *tagliolini* are completely dry.

MARIA PIA

THE LOST CUSTOM OF ADDOBBI

The University of Bologna is the oldest-surviving university in the world and is full of majestic buildings, monuments, churches and porticoes that require and receive continuous restoration. According to the old custom, *addobbi* cake is prepared in celebration of neighbourhood restoration work carried out by members of the various parishes of the city. (*Addobbi* literally means decorations.) On these happy occasions, when the restoration work is finished, the obligatory cake is made – something the Italians do as a matter of course.

In Bologna the cake they make is *Torta degli addobbi*, which is made from rice and both bitter and sweet almonds. It is eaten at home, but the cake, cut into diamond shapes, was always on hand for those spontaneous social occasions. During the *addobbi*, it was once customary for people to leave their front doors unlocked so everyone they knew could come and sample the rhomboid-shaped cake.

Today, unfortunately, doors are securely padlocked – and there are even iron bars across the windows to stop people from entering when you are at home! It seems hard to believe, but it is true. Sadly, these beautiful customs of the past have been forgotten and are no longer followed because Italian society has changed so radically, and for the worse. These are signs of a society where money is all-conquering; perhaps we don't place enough value on the lives of those around us.

We should think carefully about these changes and be reminded that *Torta degli addobbi* gives us a sweetness in a special way that is no longer offered in today's society.

MARIA PIA

Torta degli addobbi
ADDOBBI CAKE

The name for this cake comes from the old Bolognese tradition described on the previous page. I made this in my Khandallah kitchen for various events I catered for, including those of the erstwhile Italian ambassador, Roberto Palmieri, so well-remembered for the splendid hospitality he extended to the city of Wellington. I always seemed to be cooking for his famous parties, to which he invited almost all the people of the city! I would like to thank Ambassador Roberto Palmieri for his generous hospitality, so typical of people from Emilia-Romagna (he is from Piacenza).

SERVES 8

1 tablespoon BUTTER for greasing tin
BREADCRUMBS
1 litre MILK
150g RICE
6 free-range, organic EGGS
200g CASTOR SUGAR
150g peeled ALMONDS
30g APRICOT KERNELS
80g CANDIED CITRON, cut into small pieces
1 cup AMARETTO liqueur
ICING SUGAR to dust

1. Butter a rectangular baking tin (30cm x 23cm) and sprinkle with breadcrumbs. Preheat the oven to 170°C.

2. Heat the milk and when it starts to boil, add the rice. Cook until all the milk is absorbed, then leave to cool.

3. Beat the eggs lightly before adding to the cooked rice. Add the sugar, almonds, apricot kernels and citron.

4. Pour in the rice mixture and spread evenly over the prepared baking tin (it should be 2.5cm high). Bake for about 30–40 minutes or until the cake becomes dry and golden on top.

5. Leave in the tin to cool. Cut into diamond shapes and pour over the amaretto. Remove one piece at a time, arrange on a serving dish and dust with icing sugar.

Maria Pia's tip: Apricot kernels are easily found in health stores.

Lo zabaione
THE HISTORY OF ZABAGLIONE CREAM

Zabaglione is a simple dessert, but one with a fascinating culinary and linguistic history. One theory is that the Italian word *zabaione* possibly derives from the Latin *sabaia*, which was a type of beer. The similarity lies not just in its colour, which is a clear yellow, but also because it has a slight froth. However, another story of how the sweet got its name is much more interesting. It is linked to Saint Pasquale of Baylon, the patron saint of cooks. The saint's day is celebrated every 17 May, particularly in Turin at the church of San Tommaso in via Pietro Micca. This is where the Guild of Cooks and Pastry Chefs was once situated. I would love to be able to honour this day here in New Zealand, so that all cooks here could join me in celebrating with a festival of food.

Saint Pasquale of Baylon lived from 1540 to 1592. He was a friar in the Third Franciscan order, which originated in Spain. He undertook various pilgrimages through Europe and ended up in Turin. As well as being a man of the church he was a brilliant cook, although he never ran a restaurant and never judged the culinary efforts of others! He was, in short, a spiritual man, inclined towards bringing peace as opposed to disorder. Being able to visit the kitchens of European courts gave him the chance to learn many of their secrets. Amongst these was the recipe for a cream as delicious as it is energising. This is the stuff of legends!

To the many women who came to him for confession, he gave advice not only on spiritual life, but also on practical matters. This, it would seem, included some recipes to strengthen wavering marriages, or to revitalise those that had become a little tired.

The most useful of the recipes in this respect was always *zabaione*. The penitents confided the recipe to their friends, and so the recipe was dispersed through word of mouth until it became inexorably linked to the name of their confessor and benefactor. In the Piedmont dialect the dessert is called *sambajon*, from the surname of the friar (Baylon). The similarity of the sounds would seem to indicate beyond doubt that the word originates from his name – except for the fact he was made a saint in 1690, nearly 100 years after his death!

So it is therefore difficult to be entirely sure who invented this dessert, although there are good reasons to think it came from the kitchens of the Court of the Duke of Savoy, Carlo Emanuele I, in the 16th century. Pasquale of Baylon would have acquired the secret during his visits there. This seems to me the most likely explanation.

However, the first written evidence of a dessert made with fresh eggs, sugar and white wine is found a century later in the recipe book *L'arte di ben cucinare* – (*The Art of Good Cookery*) – by Bartolomeo Stefani, head cook of the Gonzaga family in

Mantua in the mid-17th century. But the word *zabaione* could also derive from the words in the Emilian dialect for 'mix' and 'measure' – *zabui* and *bigliare*.

In Lombardy a similar dish is prepared – *la rossumada*, or *rusumada*. The difference is that while *zabaione* is prepared by heating the ingredients, *rossamuda* is simpler to prepare, as the eggs, sugar and wine are mixed without heating them. Either red or white wine can be used, depending on what is at hand; and for those unable to afford wine, even water or milk can be used. It is served in a special glass comprising a top with a built-in whisk (I unearthed one from a second-hand dealer in Milan). You stir it as you drink from it.

In Lombardy there is another hot drink (once served with coffee, like *rossamuda* and *barbajade di cioccolata*) called *sapajean*; whole eggs and sugar are beaten and then boiled with good-quality red wine. A few drops of lemon juice are added and the drink is served in a cup.

One thing is certain: *zabaione* is definitely not the creation of a French chef. (At last the French have given us credit for something, as it is claimed too often that we Italians copy from them!) Even the authoritative *Larousse Gastronomique* confirms that the French *sabajon* comes from the Italian. Regardless of its origins, *zabaione* is a great energy-giving drink. In fact, one portion of *zabaione*, without any biscuits or anything else eaten with it, comes to about 200 calories! The energy comes from the egg yolks, which contain essential amino acids as well as calcium, iron, sulphur, potassium and above all, phosphorus and vitamins, including the valuable vitamin A. The sugar also provides energy that the body uses straight away, while the small amount of alcohol contained in the wine acts as a mild stimulant.

It is hardly surprising that in times gone by grandmothers would intuitively think of *zabaione* as much more than a dessert for those with a sweet tooth (like some of my customers who specifically ask me to make it when they come to my *trattoria*). They would offer it as an ideal food for lagging children, for students under the stress of exams, or for anyone who needs a general pick-me-up.

Ricetta classica dello zabaione
CLASSIC *ZABAGLIONE*

To ensure the *Zabaglione* rises, the eggs must be very fresh and the yolks separated without any egg white whatsoever. A properly beaten *Zabaglione* should do what we Italians call *scriverà* – that is, if you let it drizzle from the whisk it should sit on the surface of the creamy mass before being absorbed.

SERVES 6

4 large free-range, organic EGG YOLKS
90g CASTOR SUGAR
90ml DRY MARSALA WINE

1. Put the egg yolks in a bowl (preferably copper), then add the sugar and Marsala wine. Place the bowl in a heated bain-marie or double-boiler (to about 75°C), kept on a moderate heat, and beat with an electric or hand whisk, increasing the speed of the rotations until the mixture becomes clear, fluffy and smooth.

2. Pour into dessert glasses and serve with biscuits. Serve hot, lukewarm or cold, or even with the addition of whipped cream.

Dolci siciliani e un po di storia legata a questa isola di Sicilia a me tanto cara!

SICILIAN SWEETS & SOME OF THE HISTORY OF THIS ISLAND THAT I LOVE SO WELL!

Tomasi di Lampedusa's novel *Il Gattopardo (The Leopard)* is a book I never tire of reading. Published in November 1957, it was an overnight success. Four editions were published in three months, followed by dozens of others – and who says Italians don't read! A film based on the novel was made in 1963, with Burt Lancaster, a young Frenchman named Alain Delon (who became famous as a result) and the quintessentially Italian Claudia Cardinale.

My father was an early devotee of this book, and to celebrate the success both of the book and its writer (who died a few months before publication) he organised a splendid party which reproduced almost all the servings described in Chapter Six, 'The Ball'. In *The Leopard*, Tomasi di Lampedusa narrates, through the goings-on of an aristocratic Palermo family, the arrival in Sicily of the *mille*, or 'the thousand'. This was the expedition of 1089 volunteer soldiers under the command of General Giuseppe Garibaldi, who brought about the fall of The Kingdom of the Two Sicilies (a political entity formed in 1812 consisting of the kingdoms of Sicily and Naples) through the annexation and unification of the island, which led to the formation of the Kingdom of Italy.

In Sicily, from 6 May to 8 November 1860, Garibaldi commanded 'the thousand', who passed into history as those who unified Italy, and who took the name Garibaldini because of the audacity and courage they displayed in their role in creating the new state.

The author of *The Leopard* wanted above all to portray the luxurious environment and uselessness of high society in The Kingdom of the Two Sicilies. The entire sixth chapter is devoted to the ball organised in November 1862 in the Pantaleone Palace in Palermo, in honour of the grand families of the city. The buffet is enormous; in fact, there are two buffets. One consisted of savoury dishes and the other comprised sweets, which the Prince of Salina, Don Fabrizio, a key character in the novel, was particularly fond.

There are two general types of sweets presented – the foreign ones (in large part French), and, much more interestingly, the typically Sicilian ones. The foreign desserts include *Beignet Dauphine,* profiteroles covered in chocolate and three types of parfait (pink ices, champagne ices and pineapple ices). But together with these foreign sweets there sits the *Babà*, a type of yeast cake soaked in rum (commonly known as *rum baba*) 'resplendent like the mane of a stallion'. I liked this expression so much I once had a dream in which I had a vision of a horse made entirely from *babà*. There is Mont Blanc, snowed with cream; the monumental *Trionfi di Gola* (Triumphs of Gluttony); and virgins' cakes, which evoke the martyrdom of Sant'Agata, whose executioner had sliced off her breasts. In fact, the Prince of Salina, the most important character in the book, pays most attention to this recipe, which in Sicilian dialect is called *Minni di Vergini* – virgins' breasts. It is a mixture of pistachio nuts and cinnamon covered by a small dome of baked egg whites.

Sicilian sweets have four fundamental ingredients: almonds, honey, pistachio nuts and strong ricotta cheese made from goats' milk. The Arabs had tried to cultivate sugar cane and rice in Sicily, but both attempts failed because of the arid growing conditions. But their teachings were fundamentally important – even today certain traditional sweets have Arab roots, such as *cassata* which comes from *qu'asat* (meaning round bowl); *cubbaita*, from *quabbayt* which is the nougat from sesame seeds; and *sorbetto* from *sciarbath*.

Many Sicilian sweets were also made in the monasteries. The sisters, the novices, and even the Venerated Mother Superior all dedicated hours and hours not only to meditation and prayer, but also to an assortment of practical activities. Out of this was born something that gained a much wider appreciation – *pasta reale*, royal marzipan, made from almonds and sugar. It was destined to transcend the borders of Sicily and spread throughout Italy, including Puglia where the use of almond paste is still widespread, especially with Easter lamb.

MARIA PIA

I was still a little girl when my parents took me up the long staircase from the Piazza Bellini in Palermo to the door of the Santa Caterina convent where the nuns of the Closet order dispensed sweets. The environment was austere but, for me, fascinating and of another era. A small room was divided in two, with a grille separating the nuns of the cloister from those of us who came from the outside world. We ordered some sweets, and the next day an incredible tray was delivered to us. The production of sweets was important for the nuns, as it brought money to the religious communities and assisted their development. Nevertheless, production reached such levels as to create concern among the church authorities, who worried about the amount of time it took the nuns away from prayer.

The most celebrated of these Sicilian pastry shops was that of Convento Palermitano, a medieval convent founded by Eloisa Martorana. Even today, the sweets of the Martorano remain the quintessence of Sicilian pastrycraft. The name Martorano is associated with the old-fashioned methods, known only to a few, where no machines are used to make sweets. *Pasta reale* was used, consisting of almonds, sugar, and natural food colouring to make identical copies of fruit and other types of food. Examples include the simple cherry, as well as apricots, peaches, small apples and, for expert sweet makers, figs with the skins opened so the red inside can be seen. Those were the ones I preferred as a child. The newest *pasta reale* inventions on display in the windows of Palermo pastry shops include such things as fake panini stuffed with salami, mock pizzas, shrimp, mussels, clams – all made of almonds and sugar!

Unfortunately *pasta reale* has two major drawbacks – it is very filling, and it is very expensive. But *pasta reale* is not the only ingredient synonymous with the art of Sicilian desserts: there are also *cannoli*. These are tubes of sweet pastry crust, almost the colour of antique bronze, filled with a mixture of ricotta, sugar, small pieces of candied fruit and chocolate, and elegantly sprinkled with ground pistachio nuts at the ends. The convents once also used to make *cannoli*; they were very big and called the *Cannoli della Zia Monaca*, which literally means Aunty Nun's *Cannoli*. The church presented these as gifts to the benefactors of the convent, and if the benefactor was particularly generous a *Cappello del turco* or Turk's hat was given. This was a large turban-shaped sweet that was

absolutely groaning with stuffed *cannoli* nestled in its folds. Only the old noble families knew these ancient customs, which have long since disappeared. I count myself fortunate to still remember them.

From the same sisters in the monasteries there was another sweet that has since disappeared, with only an easier version now in existence. This is the *Trionfi di Gola* or Triumphs of Gluttony, referred to in *The Leopard*. It was long held in high esteem in the old traditions at the Sicilian monasteries – they all had their own version of the recipe, but the first and proudest originates from the convent of Orsiglione in Palermo. My grandmother, Donna Luisa Santese Valentini, received this rarest Sicilian sweet as a gift from the convent when I was baptised. (In fact, my godparents were actually Palermitan nobles.)

Trionfi di Gola is an enormous creation made of sponge cake, soaked in sweet liqueurs, filled with custard and pistachio marmalade and iced in *pasta reale*. A calorie bomb! It was an enormous cake and took at least eight people several days to prepare. Its surrogate, or the modern version, is the *Cassata Siciliana*. The principal ingredient is ricotta, worked for a long time with sugar and liqueurs until it becomes soft and smooth. Into this is immersed the indispensable candied fruit and drops of chocolate. A mound is made with layers of sliced sponge cake with the ricotta mixture spread between each layer, followed by a topping of *pasta reale* from pistachio marzipan (the green colour cannot be dispensed with because it is the fundamental characteristic of this sweet). The cake is decorated with a lot of candied fruit in the form of roses and geometric shapes. It is a massive and very sweet cake that some adore, while others, less fond of such intense sweets, can find it rather overwhelming.

It would seem that the richness of ingredients and presentation of the Sicilian pastries was devised to be a core element of formal dining, of balls and banquets, and was exclusive to noble palaces. But perhaps this was not necessarily so. Sicilians also love fried sweets, such as the pancakes known as *sfinci*, which are filled with cream or honey, or only sugar. These are sweets made with humble ingredients, but big on flavour.

Cannoli alla Siciliana
FILLED SICILIAN PASTRY ROLLS

The best way to make cannoli is with tin forms called *scorze*. Alternatively, you can use tubes of bamboo approximately 2cm in diameter, cut into 13cm lengths.

SERVES 18

2 teaspoons bitter COCOA
2 teaspoons ESPRESSO COFFEE
2 tablespoons CASTOR SUGAR
300g FLOUR
30g BUTTER
6–7 tablespoons DRY WHITE WINE
a pinch of SALT
ALMOND OIL for brushing the forms
1 EGG WHITE
1 litre pure OLIVE OIL for frying

for the filling
400g fresh RICOTTA CHEESE,
strained through a sieve
200g ICING SUGAR
2 tablespoons HONEY
5 drops of ORANGE-FLOWER WATER
30g CANDIED ORANGE
and CITRON, chopped
30g pieces bitter CHOCOLATE
80g shelled PISTACHIOS, chopped

1. Mix all the filling ingredients together, except the pistachios, and refrigerate for 1 hour.

2. To make the *cannoli* pastry, mix the cocoa, coffee, sugar, flour, butter, wine and salt together to produce a soft dough. Add some extra white wine if the pastry is too dry. Cover and leave for 1 hour in a cool place (but not in the refrigerator).

3. Roll out the dough to a thickness of 3mm. Cut 8cm circular discs and flatten with a rolling pin to make oval shapes.

4. Brush the *cannoli* forms with almond oil, then wrap the pastry ovals around the forms to make the *cannoli*, sealing them well with a little egg white to prevent them from opening when they are cooked.

5. Leaving them on their forms, fry in oil over a medium heat. Immerse 2 cannoli at a time, removing them as soon as they turn a golden colour. Drain on absorbent paper.

6. After no more than a few minutes, use your hands or a white cloth to remove the *cannoli* from the forms. Oil the form again and repeat with new batches until the pastry is used up.

7. A few minutes before serving, fill the *cannoli* with the chilled ricotta mixture, sprinkling the outside with the pistachios.

Zuppa Inglese
THE DUKE'S TRIFLE

Tradition has it that this recipe was created by Sienese cooks in honour of the Duke of Correggio. My second daughter, Dara, was born in this beautiful city on the Po plain of Emilia-Romagna. This recipe was given to me by a woman who gave birth to a boy on the same day (July 2, 1990) in the same hospital. It is also known, however, that *Zuppa Inglese* became popular in Florence during the 18th century. It used to be served in a fantastic, old-fashioned café (since closed) named Caffè Doney and was a favourite amongst the expatriate English community which has existed in Florence for over two centuries.

There are many versions of this sweet. In Tuscany the trifle is made with both egg and chocolate custard, streaked crimson with a mixture of a liqueur known as Alchermes and the crushed shells of a type of ladybird (*cochinella* in Italian). The liqueur, which supposedly has aphrodisiac qualities, is made by monks of Saint Mark's monastery. Since the liqueur is impossible to find in New Zealand, I substitute it with a mixture of rum and cassis.

SERVES 10

for the white pastry cream (*crema pasticciera bianca*)
4 large free-range, organic EGG YOLKS
150g CASTOR SUGAR
50g WHITE FLOUR
20g POTATO FLOUR
650ml MILK
1 VANILLA POD
zest of 1 LEMON (in a single piece)
350ml FULL CREAM for whipping
50ml RUM

for the chocolate cream
150g dark CHOCOLATE
20g BUTTER
2 tablespoons MILK
2 tablespoons RUM

for the base
100ml CASSIS (blackcurrant liqueur)
30ml RUM
5 tablespoons WATER
22–25 SPONGE FINGERS

fresh BERRY FRUIT for garnishing

MARIA PIA

to make the white pastry cream:

1. In a saucepan, whisk the egg yolks and sugar together until the sugar is completely dissolved. In a separate bowl, sift the flour and potato flour together. Add to the egg mixture, a little at a time.

2. In another saucepan, put the milk, vanilla pod and whole lemon zest and cook over a low heat, ensuring the milk does not boil. Whisk the milk into the egg mixture and cook over a low heat for 5–6 minutes until thickened, stirring constantly to prevent lumps from forming.

3. Remove the lemon zest and vanilla and pour half the pastry cream into a glass or ceramic bowl, cover with plastic wrap to prevent a skin from forming on top and set aside to cool.

4. When the pastry cream has cooled, whip the cream until stiff and fold into the pastry cream together with the rum.

to make the chocolate cream:

1. Melt the chocolate in a bain-marie or double-boiler with the butter and milk. Stir well and add the rum.

2. Add the chocolate mixture to the remaining pastry cream and return to a low heat. Cook for 3 minutes, stirring constantly. Transfer to a bowl and cover with plastic wrap.

to assemble the trifle:

1. Mix the cassis, rum and water in a bowl.

2. Break the sponge fingers into pieces and dip into the cassis mixture, a few at a time. Place in the bottom of 10 individual dessert bowls.

3. Add a layer of the white pastry cream followed by more pieces of sponge fingers and a layer of chocolate cream. Finish with a few pieces of sponge fingers and garnish with fresh berry fruit. Chill and serve.

Maria Pia's tip: For the white pastry cream, cornflour or other types of thickener can be used instead of the potato flour.

Panforte alla cannella
CINNAMON *PANFORTE*

Panforte is a dense fruit-and-nut cake that is almost synonymous with the beautiful Tuscan city of Siena. It is also one of those sweets for which everyone has their own recipe. When I was working in Florence at the macrobiotic restaurant called Apriti Sesamo (Open Sesame), I met Gianna Nannini. She was a famous singer of my generation and belongs to the equally famous family from Siena who has for centuries run the *Pasticceria Nannini*. I really don't know how many varieties of *panforte* they have made – possibly more than 50 – but the cinnamon version has always been my favourite.

Try to source the best candied citron that you can. Known in Italian as *cedro* and imported from Sicily, it is green and has an entirely unique flavour. In Wellington we are fortunate to have the wonderful Nut Store on Cuba Street, owned by David Upchurch and Alison Sandle. I began using their ingredients when I opened Maria Pia's and have never once been let down by the quality of their products. *Panforte* keeps for months if wrapped in foil.

SERVES 8

1 tablespoon BUTTER for greasing tin
250g peeled, whole ALMONDS
200g WALNUTS
100g PISTACHIO NUTS, shelled
150g small soft, dried, Turkish FIGS
300g top-quality CANDIED CITRON FRUIT PEEL
2 teaspoons ground CINNAMON, plus 1 extra teaspoon for garnishing
1/2 teaspoon ground NUTMEG
70g unsweetened COCOA powder
2 tablespoons PLAIN FLOUR
100g clear HONEY
150g ICING SUGAR, plus extra for dusting the cake
RICE PAPER for lining the baking pan

1. Butter a shallow 24cm cake tin. Preheat the oven to 180°C.

2. Bake the almonds, walnuts and pistachios at 200°C for 3–4 minutes on cooking sheets. Allow to cool, then chop finely. Chop the figs and citron peel and add to the chopped nuts with the spices, cocoa powder and flour.

3. Dissolve the honey and icing sugar in a double-boiler and cook for 8–10 minutes, or longer if necessary, until it forms a hardened thread when drizzled from a spoon. Stir into the dry ingredients.

4. Spoon the mixture into the prepared cake tin. Smooth the surface and cover with a layer of rice paper cut to size. Bake for 40 minutes.

5. Allow to cool and dust with the extra cinnamon and icing sugar.

Erbazzone dolce
SWEET RICOTTA & SPINACH CAKE

My husband Richard and I lived in Modena just after we married in 1986. There I discovered the amazing generosity of the Emiliani, not to mention their connection with their land and the quality of their food products, so famous around the world. This is a classic sweet from Emilia-Romagna district. It is better to prepare the pastry for this cake a day in advance or the evening before, as it will be lighter and more crumbly.

SERVES 8

for the filling
300g RICOTTA CHEESE
850g fresh SPINACH, cooked, drained and chopped (to yield 300g cooked spinach)
4 tablespoons HONEY
150g SUGAR
7 AMARETTI BISCUITS, finely ground
150g ground ALMONDS
50g ground WALNUTS
1 teaspoon CINNAMON

for the pastry
350g WHITE FLOUR
a pinch of SALT
1 teaspoon ALTERNATIVE BAKING POWDER (see glossary)
100g CASTOR SUGAR
2 EGG YOLKS
200g BUTTER, softened to room temperature
1/2 cup SAMBUCA

1 EGG YOLK and 1 tablespoon WATER for brushing
1 cup SAMBUCA

to make the filling:
1. In a bowl, mix the ricotta cheese, spinach, honey, sugar, amaretti biscuits, almonds, walnuts and cinnamon.

to make the pastry:
1. Sift the flour, salt and baking powder together. Form a mound with a crater in the centre. Add the sugar, egg yolks and butter. Using a fork and knife rather than your hands mix all the ingredients well. Add the Sambuca and, if necessary, a bit of water to moisten.
2. Make a ball and cover in plastic wrap and place in the refrigerator overnight.

to assemble the cake:
1. Preheat oven to 170°C.
2. Line the base and sides of a 26cm round baking tin with non-stick baking paper. Using your fingers press three-quarters of the pastry into the dish leaving a 2cm overlap all around.

3. Add the filling and spread evenly as this is essential to the process. Brush the edges of the pastry with the beaten egg yolk and water.

4. Roll out the remaining pastry dough and cut into strips. Arrange in a criss-cross pattern over the filling and brush with the egg-yolk mixture.

5. Bake for 45–50 minutes in the centre of the oven.

6. Remove from the oven, sprinkle over the Sambuca and allow to cool.

Torta di nocciole e noci al cioccolato
HAZELNUT & WALNUT CHOCOLATE CAKE

SERVES 8

250g WHITE FLOUR

2 teaspoons ALTERNATIVE BAKING POWDER (see glossary)

50g DARK CHOCOLATE

2 pinches SALT

3 tablespoons VINCOTTO

3 tablespoons strong black COFFEE (short black)

3 tablespoons MILK

100g BUTTER

2 large free-range, organic EGGS, separated

100g WALNUTS, soaked in water overnight, finely chopped

50 HAZELNUTS, toasted and finely chopped

1/4 teaspoon CREAM OF TARTAR

ICING SUGAR for sprinkling

1. Line the base of a 23cm round cake tin with non-stick baking paper. Preheat the oven to 180°C.

2. Sift the flour, baking powder and pinch of salt into a bowl. Repeat several times to ensure that it is evenly mixed.

3. In a bain-marie or double-boiler, mix the chocolate, vincotto, coffee, milk and butter. Mix well until melted. Remove from the heat and mix in the egg yolks.

4. Place the walnuts and hazelnuts in a bowl. Add the chocolate mixture and the flour mixture a little at a time until well mixed.

5. In a separate bowl beat the egg whites, cream of tartar and pinch of salt until stiff. Fold into the chocolate mixture very carefully and pour into the prepared cake tin.

6. Bake for 25 minutes or until a toothpick inserted into the centre comes out clean. Remove from the oven and allow to cool for 30 minutes. Sprinkle with icing sugar and serve.

Africanetti o spumette di mandorle e nocciole
'LITTLE AFRICANS' OR ALMOND & HAZELNUT MERINGUES

This classic Pugliese sweet is perfect for accompanying a cup of coffee or tea. It also goes beautifully with strong cheeses such as gorgonzola.

MAKES APPROXIMATELY 25 MERINGUES

5 free-range, organic **EGG WHITES**
500g **DEMERARA SUGAR**
a pinch of **SALT**
450g **ALMONDS**, toasted and finely chopped
50g **HAZELNUTS**, roughly chopped

1. Fill a conventional muffin tin with paper baking cups (5cm diameter). Preheat the oven to 100°C.

2. Beat the egg whites with the sugar and a pinch of salt until stiff. Fold in the almonds and hazelnuts.

3. Spoon the mixture into each baking cup, filling them almost to the top.

4. Bake for 25–30 minutes until the surface is golden brown.

Biscottini di Marzapane
MARZIPAN COOKIES

MAKES APPROXIMATELY 40 COOKIES

1 tablespoon **BUTTER** for greasing tin
1 tablespoon **FLOUR** for dusting tin
500g blanched **ALMONDS**
50g **APRICOT KERNELS**
450g **CASTOR SUGAR**, plus 50g for coating
2 free-range, organic **EGGS**
2 teaspoons natural **VANILLA ESSENCE**
zest of 1 **LEMON**, finely grated

1. Butter and flour a baking tray. Preheat the oven to 180°C.

2. Grind the almonds and apricot kernels in a food processor until they form a fine paste.

3. Transfer to a bowl with 450g sugar, eggs, vanilla essence and lemon zest. Work this mixture with your fingers until smooth.

4. Make mixture into balls the size of walnuts and roll in the remaining sugar.

5. Arrange the balls on the baking tray and bake for 15 minutes. Allow to cool completely before serving. Serve with a sweet *digestivo* or liqueur.

Grano al vincotto e melograno
COOKED SPELT WITH VINCOTTO & POMEGRANATE

A version of this sweet can be found in most middle-eastern cultures with more or less the same name as used in my region of Puglia: *colua* or *colla*. In Greece it is known as *kolliva*. In the northern hemisphere it is typically made in the autumn, as this is the time of the year when pomegranates are plentiful.

SERVES 8

300g uncooked SPELT WHEAT
1 large POMEGRANATE
150g WALNUTS, soaked overnight
150g dark CHOCOLATE, cut into small pieces
100g CANDIED ORANGE or CITRON
1 tablespoon ground CINNAMON
5 tablespoons VINCOTTO
juice of 1 ORANGE

1. Soak the spelt in a large bowl in cold water for two nights, changing the water 2–3 times (alternately you can used tinned, cooked spelt or *farro*, available from specialty food shops).

2. Drain the spelt and place in a pressure cooker. Cover with water to 5cm over the spelt. Bring to pressure and reduce the heat. Cook for one and a half hours. Remove from the heat, cover with a towel and let the pressure cooker cool down.

3. When cool, transfer the spelt to a large ceramic bowl, mixing in all of the remaining ingredients.

4. Serve in small bowls, garnished with fresh pomegranate seeds.

CHAPTER NINE

Alla ricerca dell'elisir di lunga vita
LIQUEURS AND ELIXIRS OF LONG LIFE

When I lived and cooked in Tuscany, one of my most valuable discoveries was when I visited the monasteries, abbeys and convents to sample their various elixirs, liqueurs and *amari* or *digestivi*. Monks, and sometimes also nuns, have a long tradition of making these with secret recipes. As the saying goes, *Ora et labora* . . . pray and work . . .

It is an Italian tradition to prepare homemade liqueurs and *rosolio* to offer to guests. (My mother, Gilda Valentini, made one called *perlei*.) The idea, quite simply, is that following a meal your guests would remain in your home to enjoy a *digestivo* and some good conversation. This to me seems a much better alternative than 'going out for a drink'.

Abbeys and monasteries have traditionally always been built in magnificent hermit-like locations. They were ideally situated close to hundreds of varieties of herbs, roots and flowers, many of which had medicinal properties. Elixirs and liqueurs were produced over the centuries (and still are today) in the abbeys and monasteries by the monks who were experts in alchemy, using herbs, plant roots and fruits. Even medicinal herbs were used in liqueurs. The research was begun towards the end of the 13th century by Arnaldo da Villanova, the personal doctor to Pope Boniface VIII.

It was only around 1700 that these places of alchemy, rich with arboricultural texts, that the infusion of liqueurs, *digestivi* and tonics of herbs and roots received special recognition. It was a Benedictine monk, the mythical Dom Perignon, whose name will be remembered forever, who worked in the cellars of the Abbey of Hautvilers in France and who prepared the base for what is now known as Champagne.

In the 1970s I went to visit the celebrated Abbey of Monte Oliveto Maggiore, in the province of Siena. For strategic reasons abbeys such as this were built in isolated places. It was founded by Bernardo Tolomei in 1313, an illustrious jurist who had retired to monastic life. The abbey always had an aristocratic and intellectual character and was an important centre for the arts and sciences. There is an enormous double-gallery cloister with frescoes by Signorelli, with scenes from the life of Saint Benedict.

There I discovered my favourite liqueur – *La flora di Monte Oliveto*. Each bottle is very thick and almost a unique object in itself. This liqueur is still made exclusively with natural essences and is the result of centuries of experience and a completely original way of working. It is prepared with two-thirds aromatic and medicinal herbs, skilfully measured according to an ancient recipe which of course is kept secret. The herbs are mixed in a way that offers a unique and typical flavour, and the liqueur has 38 per cent alcohol content. It is ideal both as a tonic and as a *digestivo*.

MARIA PIA

Another recipe from these friars is called *goccia amara*, consisting of gentian bark and other beneficial roots that have a bitter, dry taste. It is also a remedy for constipation.

Tre monti is a liqueur with a 48 per cent alcohol content, and is very strong with a dry taste obtained from lime-tree flowers. The lime or linden tree is a majestic tree that grows freely all over Europe. It is long-living and slow-growing. It is characterised by perfumed flowers, sought after because of their essence, which is obtained through distillation. This distillate is called *asprizia vegetale* or vegetable bitters. For years a few drops were always on my dresser. In times of famine, lime flowers were also ground and mixed with flour to make bread.

At one time, my mother was able to tell a storm was approaching when the lime flowers started to exude an intense fragrance, so intense that even the bees were stupefied by it. It is one of my favourite trees. My grandmother always planted lime trees at the entrance to her properties. According to local tradition, the lime tree is also a fertility symbol.

The 42 per cent *grappa* produced in the abbey is also exceptional, distilled from the pressings of the schiava grape and left to age for a while. And another type of *digestif* made by the monks is called *china* (pronounced 'kina'), obtained with an authentic peel of *china calisaya* and other aromatic barks. The best *china* (21 per cent) that I have ever drunk was at the same abbey. I love drinking it hot with a dash of lemon or lime on cold winter days.

Few would suspect, though, that one of the best gins in the world is produced only a few kilometres from Florence in the Casentino at Vallambrosa, in the Monastery of the Vallombrosani monks. It is not known how the monks came up with this recipe, which is a jealously guarded secret. I went there with two friends, one of them English and the other a friend from Florence, Edoardo Castorina, who was my guide. We all agreed that the gin was indeed exceptional! Around the year 1000 a young noble Florentine, Giovanni Gualberto of the powerful Visdomini, along with a few companions, founded the first communities in the forests of Vallombroso. At the time it was called *Acque Belle* – Beautiful Waters – because of the richness of its springs. Towards the end of the 15th century that religious community, which had begun with a few huts, gave birth to a grandiose monastery. Nearby there is a stupendous forest, with big trees hundreds of years old. But what fascinated me most of all was their gin and the enormous collection of books in the library.

Still near Florence, towards the south, is the powerful Certosa del Galluzzo. The Cistercian monks have one of the largest monastic distilleries in existence and produce about 15 varieties of liqueurs. Among the most famous and popular is the medicinal brandy, obtained from distilling a particular type of wine, the location of whose vines remains a closely guarded secret. The *rosolio* with mandarin is very delicate, as is *le gocce di tintura imperiale*. They are made through distilling a great number of medicinal herbs. The convent of San Benedetto and the monastery of San Giovanni Evangelista near Arezzo are also both very special.

Nowadays there are not many monks left, but they still produce a superb *nocino* using walnuts that are gathered on 24 June, the day of Saint Giovanni. They are left to infuse in alcohol until mid-August, the Feast of the Assumption. The liquid obtained is filtered, bottled and left to age in darkness for at least four or five years.

Visiting all these places inspired me to make my own liqueurs. It is important when making liqueurs to ensure that the jars or containers are always tightly sealed, otherwise the alcohol will evaporate.

Rosolio al Basilico
BASIL *ROSOLIO*

MAKES 500ML

100g BASIL leaves, washed and dried
200ml ALCOHOL
syrup of 600g SUGAR and 400ml WATER

1. Place the basil leaves and alcohol in a tightly sealed container for 120 days, shaking once a day. Strain the leaves from the alcohol.

2. Make the syrup with the sugar and water and add to the alcohol. Store in a well-sealed 1 litre bottle.

Limoncello di Maria Pia
MARIA PIA'S LEMON LIQUEUR

In Italy it is common to keep both the *limoncello* and its glasses in the freezer. If you are ever at the seaside in 40°C heat, you'll see why this liqueur is perfect! I find that alcohol heavily infused with lemon is very acidic and aids digestion after a good lunch or dinner. But do not drink *limoncello* if you have just had a cup of coffee with milk. Hawke's Bay produces some of the best lemons in New Zealand and they are great to use in this *limoncello*.

MAKES 500ML

13 LEMONS
450ml pure ALCOHOL
syrup of 350g CASTOR SUGAR and 450ml WATER

1. Immerse the lemons in 200ml of alcohol. Leave to infuse for 1 week, shaking every now and then to assist with the infusion of the aromas. Use only the yellow part of the lemon skin.

2. When ready, strain through a cloth and add a further 250ml alcohol, plus the sugar and water syrup. Bottle in either 250ml or 500ml bottles.

MARIA PIA

Liquore di alloro – di mia nonna Luisa
MY GRANDMOTHER LUISA'S BAY-LEAF LIQUEUR
MAKES 500ML

50 green, tender BAY LEAVES, washed and dried
400ml pure ALCOHOL
syrup of 250g SUGAR and 200ml WATER

1. Place the bay leaves and the alcohol in a tightly sealed container for 15 days, shaking once a day.

2. Make the syrup with the sugar and water and add to the alcohol. Strain the alcohol through a cloth, mix in the alcohol and strain again. Store in a well-sealed bottle.

Ratafia di ciliegie
CHERRY *RATAFIA* LIQUEUR

This is my favourite, which I made during the period I lived in Emilia-Romagna. The Vignola cherry (from near Modena) is famous all over the world for its sweetness. The best are those that are very ripe and succulent. I remember I was chuffed to see the change of colour day by day. This liqueur deserves to be put in an antique rococo bottle! Every year towards June I went to gather cherries of different varieties to understand how *rosolio* assumes a different flavour according to the type of cherry used. Also wild cherries are incredible to use with this recipe.

MAKES 500ML

350g ripe CHERRIES
10g CINNAMON STICKS
700ml pure ALCOHOL or GRAPPA
syrup of 700g SUGAR and 280ml WATER

1. Infuse the cherries and cinnamon in the alcohol in a tightly sealed jar for 7–10 days until the liquid turns brown. Shake often.

2. Strain through a cloth several times until clear. Mix the syrup, then add to the alcohol.

BIBLIOGRAPHY

Cucina del Salento, Giorgio Cretì, Capone Editore, 2002

Cucina Popolare e Aristocratica di Terra d'Otranto, Antonio Edoardo Foscarini, Capone Editore, 1990

Enciclopedia dei Ragazzi, Rizzoli Editore, 1992

Il Gattopardo, Giuseppe Tomasi di Lampedusa, Feltrinelli Editore, 2003

Grecìa Salentina: La Cultura Gastronomica, Pietro Manni, Manni Editore, 2001

Guida alla Macrobiotica, Cristina Tomshensky, Feltrinelli Editore, 1984

I Messapi, Cesare Daquino, Capone Editore, 1999

The Original Mediterranean Cuisine, Barbara Santich, Wakefield Press, 1995

Puglia in Tavola: Le Ricette della Tradizione, Nicola Sbisà, Adda Editore, 2004

Il Salento e la sua Civiltà, Rosella Barletta, Schena Editore, 1996

Storia della Puglia, Capone Editore, 2004

Umberto Saba, Poetry and Prose, Vincent Moleta, Bridgetown, Aeolian Press, 2004

Whole Foods Companion, Deanne Onstad, Chelsea Green Publishing Company, 1996

GLOSSARY

Apricot kernels Their bitter taste combined with other ingredients gives a sense of harmonious balance; however, they should be used sparingly.

Caciocavallo One of the most popular and widely used cow's-milk cheeses from southern Italy. Pear-shaped and typically tied with a sort of 'noose' so that it can be hung for ageing and/or smoking. The name literally means 'horse cheese' and is said to derive from the way the cheeses are tied and then hung, which is reminiscent of a rider's legs. A compact yet elastic cheese, it is ideal for cooking in that it melts quickly but holds its shape. Depending on its age, the taste can be either sweet or sharp.

Cavolo nero Known as Tuscan or black cabbage, this is a tall, leafy member of the cabbage family.

Cime di rapa Also known as *broccoli rabe*, it is distinguished by tender green leaves and small broccoli flowers. It helps cleanse the blood of toxins and is also good for controlling calcium in the body. As other members of the brassica family, this vegetable contains dithiolthiones, a substance reputed to help combat breast and colon cancer.

Fresh yeast This should be stored in the fridge and used within a week; alternatively it can be frozen. Some types of dry baking yeast may contain BHT (butylated hydroxy toluene), which is a petroleum-based antioxidant and is best avoided. In Wellington I source fresh yeast from Moore Wilson's; in Auckland it is available at Zarbo Delicatessen in Newmarket.

Raising powder (or alternative baking powder) I don't like using conventional baking powder and have found this fantastic alternative. It is free from wheat, aluminium, sodium and dairy products and is produced by Thomson's Foods, PO Box 20-414, Glen Eden, Auckland (09) 835 1223.

Taleggio This cheese has been produced in Lombardy (the region of Milan) for many centuries. It is a table cheese with a firm, creamy consistency and a light aromatic flavour. Taleggio is a washed rind cheese produced in square or rectangular forms. The outer crust is soft, thin and light golden in colour, which deepens as the cheese ages. The inside the cheese is creamy yellow. I consider it one of Italy's finest cheeses.

Vincotto An ancient form of cooked must from negramaro and malvasia grapes, cooked slowly over many hours and then filtered to obtain a dark-coloured liquid. Avoid Vincotto that contains sugar and artificial colours. In Salento almost every family makes its own Vincotto. Sometimes quince figs are added to the must to produce a different aroma.

Recipe INDEX

ACKNOWLEGEMENTS

Firstly I would like to express my deepest gratitude to my husband Richard Klein for his help with the translation and for running our restaurant, especially when I was away during my research in Puglia. The same thanks goes out to our staff, who enabled us to have our first family holiday in Italy since immigrating to New Zealand in 1997. I extend gratitude also to my two daughters, Astrid and Dara, for their suggestions on the intuitive woman's point of view.

Salvatore Criscillo for the food photography and Erin Criscillo for her valuable comments.

To Nick Ryan for the use of his classic vespa.

To Dan Williams, our financial advisor and business mentor. To Vincent Moleta for his gracious permission to quote his translation of Umberto Saba.

And to all the women who were the 'oral sources' of all the recipes – it would be difficult to name them all.

To all the customers of Maria Pia's, first in Khandallah and then at our *trattoria* in Thorndon. This book is really for all of you.

Special thanks to all the people of my land, Puglia, for the moments shared during my research in the summer of 2004 and, above all, for their optimism and support.

Penguin Books

Published by the Penguin Group
Penguin Group (NZ), cnr Airborne and Rosedale Roads, Albany,
Auckland 1310, New Zealand (a division of Pearson New Zealand Ltd)
Penguin Group (USA) Inc., 375 Hudson Street,
New York, New York 10014, USA
Penguin Group (Canada), 90 Eglinton Avenue East, Suite 700, Toronto,
Ontario, M4P 2Y3, Canada (a division of Pearson Penguin Canada Inc.)
Penguin Books Ltd, 80 Strand, London, WC2R 0RL, England
Penguin Ireland, 25 St Stephen's Green,
Dublin 2, Ireland (a division of Penguin Books Ltd)
Penguin Group (Australia), 250 Camberwell Road, Camberwell,
Victoria 3124, Australia (a division of Pearson Australia Group Pty Ltd)
Penguin Books India Pvt Ltd, 11, Community Centre,
Panchsheel Park, New Delhi 110 017, India
Penguin Books (South Africa) (Pty) Ltd, 24 Sturdee Avenue,
Rosebank, Johannesburg 2196, South Africa

Penguin Books Ltd, Registered Offices: 80 Strand, London, WC2R 0RL, England

First published in 2005
1 3 5 7 9 10 8 6 4 2

Copyright © text, Maria Pia de Razza and Richard Klein 2005
Copyright © food photography Sal Criscillo
Copyright © additional photography Andrea Morgante, Saul Sonzogni,
Maria Francesca Te Huki and the de Razza-Klein family albums.

The right of Maria Pia de Razza to be identified as the author of this work in terms
of section 96 of the Copyright Act 1994 is hereby asserted.

Designed and typeset by Athena Sommerfeld
Printed by Wai Man Book Binding, China

ISBN 0 14 302054 4
A catalogue record for this book is available from the National Library of New Zealand.

www.penguin.co.nz

MARIA PIA